ARTURO HERRERA

Les Noces (The Wedding)

Visual Arts of the Americas
Modern and Contemporary Publication Series

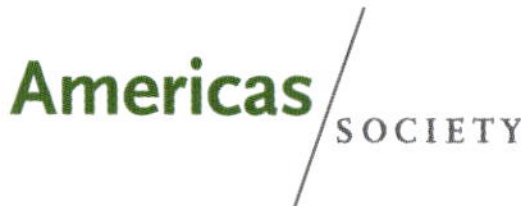

Americas Society gratefully acknowledges the following donors for their generous support of this exhibition: Chevron, Mercantil, Daniel and Estrellita Brodsky, and Maria Cristina and Pablo Henning.

We also thank Sikkema Jenkins & Co. for their in-kind support and collaboration.

Americas Society's Visual Arts Program is supported by Sharon Schultz Simpson and in part by public funds from the New York City Department of Cultural Affairs in partnership with the City Council.

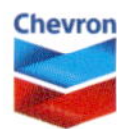

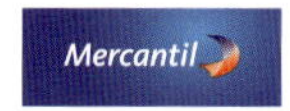

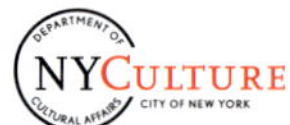

EXHIBITION CURATOR AND PUBLICATION EDITOR
Gabriela Rangel

ASSISTANT EDITORS
Christina De León
Isabela Villanueva

RESEARCH ASSISTANT
Natalie Bunnel

COPYEDITOR
Marcie Muscat

EXHIBITION AND PUBLICATION DESIGNER
Kate Johnson

PHOTOGRAPHER
Arturo Sánchez

ISBN: 978-1-879128-38-5

Published by Americas Society
680 Park Avenue, New York, NY 10065

Printed in China by Midas Printing
Distributed by D.A.P./ Distributed Art Publishers, Inc.

FOREWORD

For more than forty years Americas Society's mission has been to foster a deeper understanding of the significant cultural production occurring throughout the Western hemisphere. One of the ways the organization has furthered this goal is through its longstanding commitment to presenting exhibitions, which focus on artistic practices that deserve greater attention in the United States. *Arturo Herrera: Les Noces* (The Wedding) curated by Visual Arts Director Gabriela Rangel, is an extraordinary addition to this legacy. Centered on the two-channel digital projection *Les Noces* (2007) by the Venezuelan-born, Berlin-based artist Arturo Herrera, the exhibition also includes nine additional works of varying mediums that illuminated almost twenty years of artistic process.

Herrera has journeyed through his career employing a discourse of abstraction and modernist history, which manifests itself in the inventive and, at times, subtle ways in which he uses collage. *Untitled* (2004) is a series of eighty black-and-white photographs taken by the

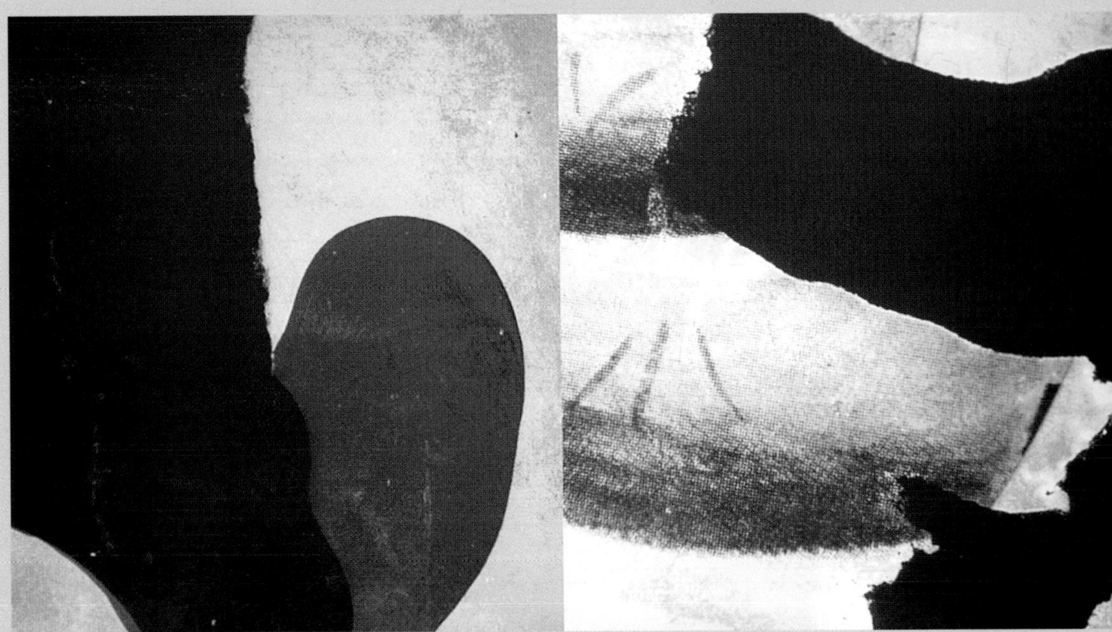

Stills from Arturo Herrera's digital projection *Les Noces*, 2007. Photograph by Arturo Sánchez

artist of scraps of materials and unfinished artworks lying around his studio. Using photographic lenses, Herrera created an assemblage of manipulated forms, textures, and images to produce a work that would ultimately serve as the basis for *Les Noces.* Herrera then worked with a computer programmer to create a software system that draws from his library of images the source material for the two-screen digital projection. The images move randomly to the percussive pitch of Igor Stravinsky's score for *Les Noces*—a radically innovative but rarely performed ballet first presented in 1923 by the Ballets Russes in Paris.

Herrera has held a longstanding fascination with the Ballet Russes, the short-lived yet legendary dance company whose mythic founder and director, Sergei Diaghilev, was well known for working with contemporary composers and artists to create extraordinary scores, sets, and costumes for his productions. Some of his most notable collaborators were Georges Braque, Gabrielle Chanel, Giorgio de Chirico, Salvador Dalí, André Derain, Natalia Goncharova, Henri Matisse, Joan Miró, and Pablo Picasso, among many others. The company's cross-disciplinary approach to artistic production served as a powerful stimulus for Herrera, who through a gesture of reverence and creative ingenuity created *Les Noces*—his first work to incorporate sound and moving images.

By merging art, music, and dance history, this publication, much like the exhibition, is reflective of the cross-disciplinary efforts that continue to flourish within the arts. Americas Society is honored to include contributions by Dr. Nuit Banai, Arturo Herrera, Dr. Lynn Garafola, Dame Monica Mason, and Christopher Newton.

I wish to congratulate and extend my gratitude to Arturo Herrera, Gabriela Rangel, and the Visual Arts team—Christina De León, Arturo Sánchez, and Isabela Villanueva—as well as their dedicated interns Seth Becker and Natalie Bunnell, who together produced this successful and exciting project.

I especially thank our donors, Chevron, Mercantil, Estrellita and Daniel Brodsky, and Maria Cristina and Pablo Henning, for their generous support of this exhibition and catalogue, as well as Sikkema Jenkins & Co. for in-kind support and collaboration. We are also grateful to Sharon Schultz Simpson and the New York City Department of Cultural Affairs in partnership with the City Council for their support of the Visual Arts Program.

SUSAN L. SEGAL
PRESIDENT AND CEO, AMERICAS SOCIETY

ARTURO HERRERA'S *LES NOCES* AND THE UNFATHOMABLE QUALITY OF FRAGMENTS

GABRIELA RANGEL

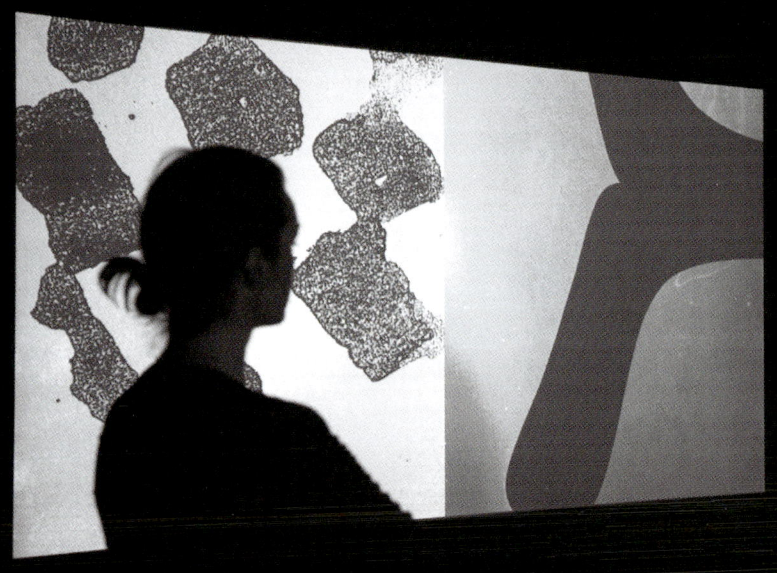

Arturo Herrera's digital projection *Les Noces* at Americas Society Art Gallery, 2011. Photograph by Arturo Sánchez

IMPURE ABSTRACTION

Over twenty years, Arturo Herrera has devoted himself to mastering a working method that allows him to adapt the history of abstraction and the myths that surround it to the liminal conditions of representation in the post-nation-state, particularly through his use of collage as a montage technique in which fragments of reality and everyday scrap materials are affixed to a two-dimensional surface. Collage is, fundamentally, a process by which the limits imposed by the binary distinctions of painting and sculpture—or, indeed, of fiction and reality—are overcome. Such a break with convention is achieved through the insertion of fragments that introduce multiple and alternate realities. Arguments for Herrera's recovery of the traditionally expressive possibilities of collage through his unusual combination of materials and use of strategies of representation that oppose the concept of waste have previously been put forth by a number of scholars.[1] I would add here that the artist has, in fact, succeeded in expanding upon these basic principles, adding multivalent layers of meaning to his works through the application of preexisting materials and discarded objects.

Unlike Carlos Cruz-Diez, Alejandro Otero, and Jesús Rafael Soto—the foundational triad of Venezuelan kinetic and geometrical abstract artists—whose designation of origin and all-encompassing narratives converged on the nation-state, Herrera's practice is put forward "along the borders of cultural integration"—that is, in the interstitial space formed by the amalgamation of trades and knowledge that result from the "process of transcultural negotiation."[2] Living in Chicago and New York, and, more recently, in Berlin, Herrera has since the 1990s been developing a body of work in which myriad comic-book characters, children's coloring books, and other mass-produced images are subjected to a process of fragmentation. The disintegration of form, incipient in his earlier works, has increased as the artist adds steps and detours to the basic process of cutting and pasting.

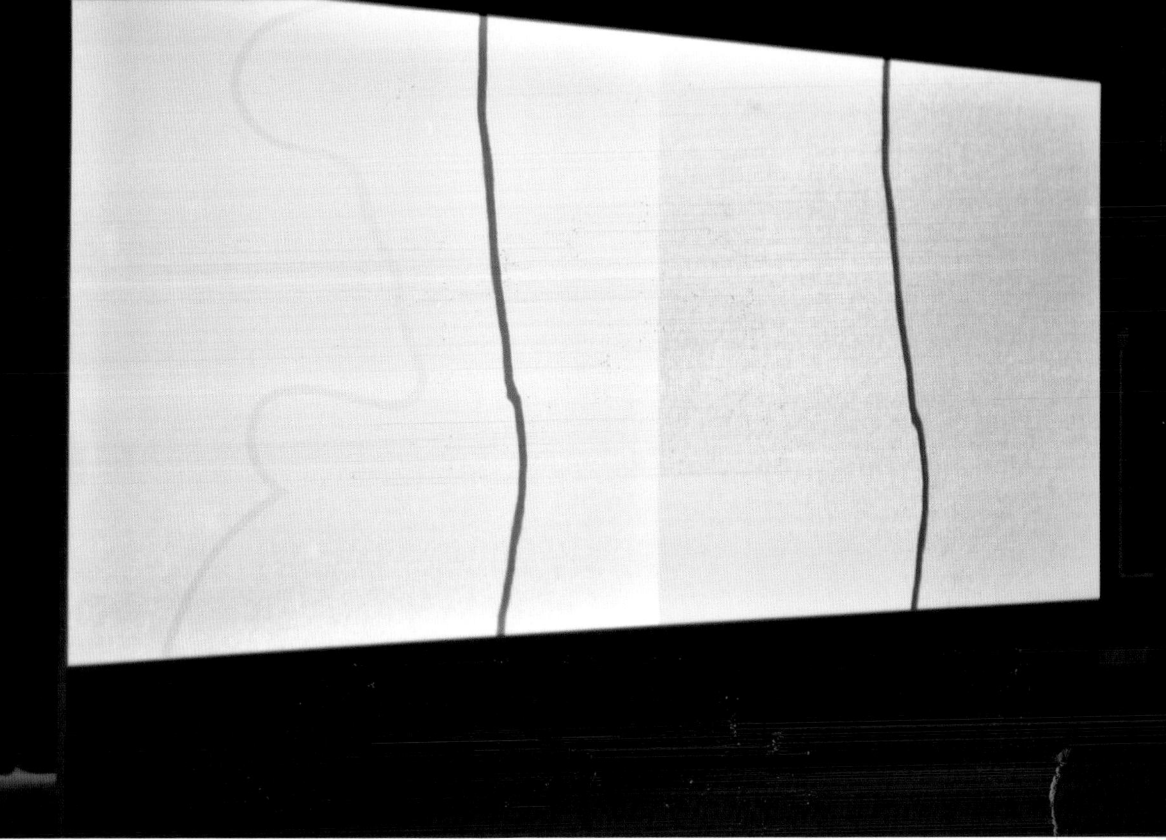

It is important to note that Herrera's work is not specific to any one medium, and he has created two-dimensional works using, among other materials, paper, felt, polyethylene, wood, wall paint, postcards, and silver-nitrate photographs, as well as sculptures in stainless steel and Formica and the digital projection *Les Noces* (2007). Herrera uses the historical process of collage as a starting point from which to elaborate upon artistic forms, which mutate from one medium to another in order to explore different aspects of the history of abstraction. In spite of their formal completeness, Herrera's works delve into the dispersion of meanings, the mixture of identities, and the viral dissemination of images as regulating principles that inform the visual arts at the present.

More interested "in the concept of abstraction,"[3] or, rather, in its archaeology, Herrera attests to the collapse and eventual disappearance of the premise of originality inherent in collage by exploring the technique's unfathomable possibilities. His excavations of such a

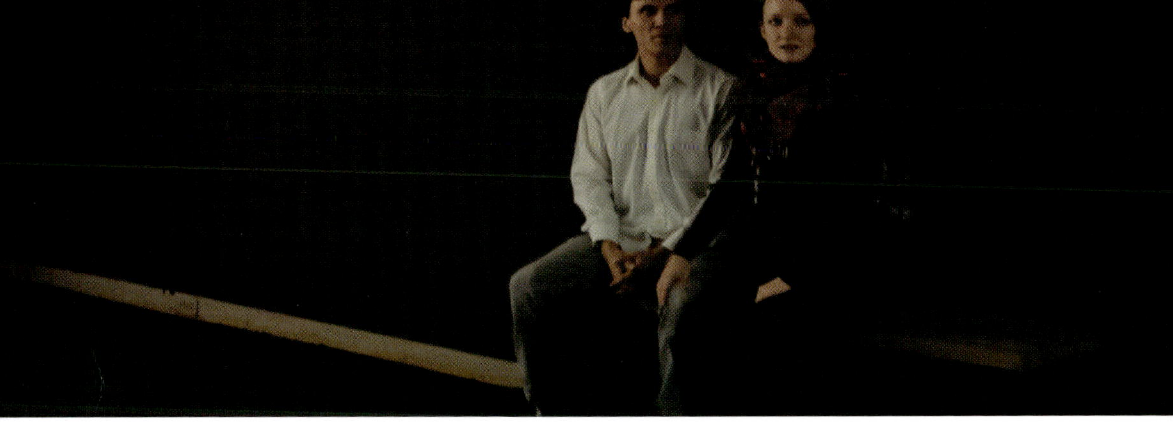

Arturo Herrera's digital projection *Les Noces* at Americas Society Art Gallery, 2011. Photograph by Arturo Sánchez

loaded tradition have given rise to bi-dimensional works comprising graphite and coffee stains superimposed onto popular motifs or comic-book characters. *Plot* (2006), a massive, flat stainless-steel piece placed at the edge of a wall, formally recalls the methods of Action Painting, adopting the anonymous horizontality of a Carl Andre sculpture (perhaps the title alludes to the props made by Richard Serra?), while its paradoxical shape might hint at the outline of Walt Disney's Bambi.[4]

Further embracing strategies of appropriation and collaboration, Herrera has enlisted the help of professional illustrators, who airbrushed settings and landscapes from animated films as backgrounds onto which the artist juxtaposed additional materials. Herrera's collages are notably organized as puzzles, and even though collage is a technique that offers the possibility of either breaking up reality or reassembling fragments into a cohesive whole, his works eschew identification or recomposition, leaving these tasks to the polymorphous imagination of the public.[5]

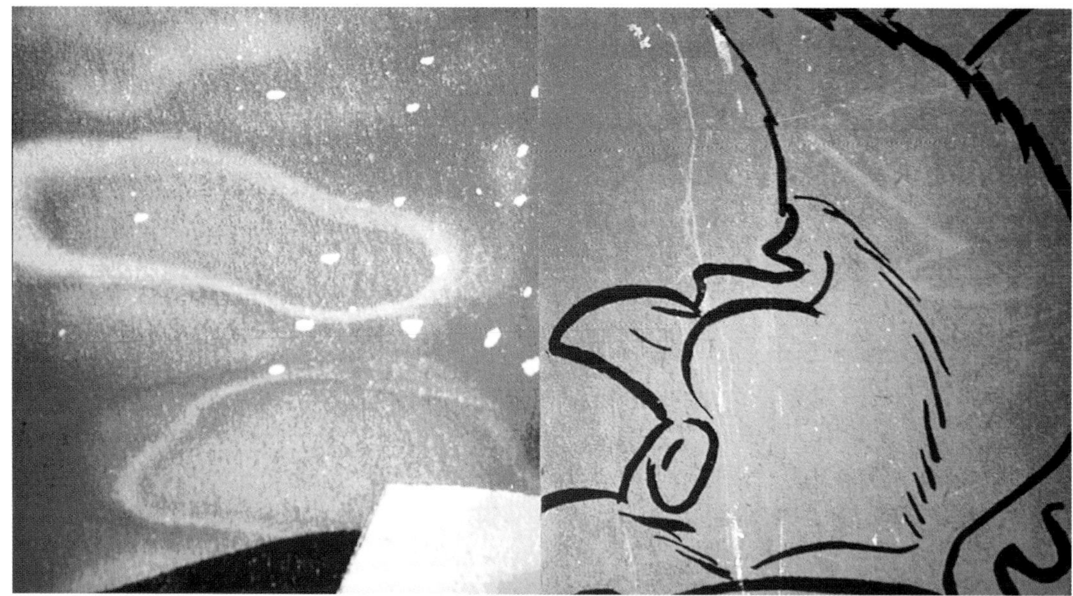

Stills from Arturo Herrera's digital projection *Les Noces*, 2007. Photograph by Arturo Sánchez

For Herrera, his practice in relation to modern art and its concomitant modernisms serves to imbue abstraction with impurity: "The X-acto knife cuts everything into little bits, fragments that I then use to create new images. These are like little bits of modernism all around me. And the fragments have this hopeful connection to some ideal from before. Dislocating and destroying elements result in a hybrid that recalls and at the same time undercuts its origins. My fragmentation provides another view of the contamination or impurity of modernism."[6] The fragments thus form sediments, layered in time in series that not only reveal the mutations and eventual destruction of the forms and motifs that Herrera has systematically catalogued but also carry out a distinctive (and differential) dissection of abstraction as a language that shows the fissures in the avant-garde's universalist aspirations. As suggested by Homi Bhabba, "cultural difference, as a form of [postcolonial] intervention," represents the process of interpretation shaped by the perplexity of living in the "disjunctive and liminal space" of the nation, erasing "the harmonious totalities of the Culture."[7]

The fragments Herrera uses to create his collages represent "cultural debris,"[8] through which the artist has configured his own archive of cultural differences within the all-encompassing narratives of modern art. The fragment, lacking authorial identity, behaves as a virus that mutates so as to undermine the narrative potential of a specific image, shape, or motif. What Herrera "fragments, dislocates, or recomposes isn't the image itself but its legibility," considering that "what moves the artist to appropriate serially produced images is the ability of the reproduction to be readily recognized and consumed by a collective audience."[9]

As T. S. Eliot wrote, "We had the experience but missed the meaning. And approach to the meaning restores the experience."[10] Although "meaning" forms part of the collective memory of an audience made dissolute through the overconsumption of images, like childhood it becomes ungraspable or lost when it becomes remote, abstruse, or illegible. However, within the society of spectacle, an approach to meaning does not restore experience. On the other hand, a collage functions as a sophisticated process that masks narrative while at the same time allowing the haptic experience to unfold, thus transforming the image into a kind of *Kammerspiel*.[11] So, while Snow White's dwarves, Bambi's hindquarters, Dumbo's ears, and many of the other motifs that have been fragmented and deconstructed by Herrera are still recognizable and, therefore, generate unconscious (and libidinal) associations from their remnants, they produce a feeling of puzzlement because they are presented as defamiliarized forms.

DISMEMBERED GESAMTKUNSTWERK

Herrera works from a vast archive of images that make reference not only to the most unknown and revealing chapters of the various modernist movements but also to banal stories and episodes of lesser narrative intensity. Over the course of two decades, this idea has developed in his work, the constituent components of which could only be compared to a book of quotations wherein the grand narratives of literature mix with mass-market fiction, philosophy, advertising, art history, and self-help texts.

Herrera's explorations of different strategies of collage have transformed this cultish and self-referential type of artwork through a more direct use of photography and video—ideal conduits for the "optical unconscious." By fusing "visual and emotional joys," these new forms of artistic media articulated a powerful collectivist utopia at the dawn of the twentieth century and caused a paradigm shift in modern art.[12] "The camera introduces us to unconscious optics as psychoanalysis does to unconscious impulses,"[13] indicated Walter Benjamin, who announced the appearance of an expert though a distracted spectator whose waning attention did not prevent intellection and analysis of the movement on the film screen.[14]

In 1998, Herrera presented a black-and-white photograph of a landscape in a solo exhibition of his work at the Renaissance Society, Chicago. The image—defined as "neither spectacular

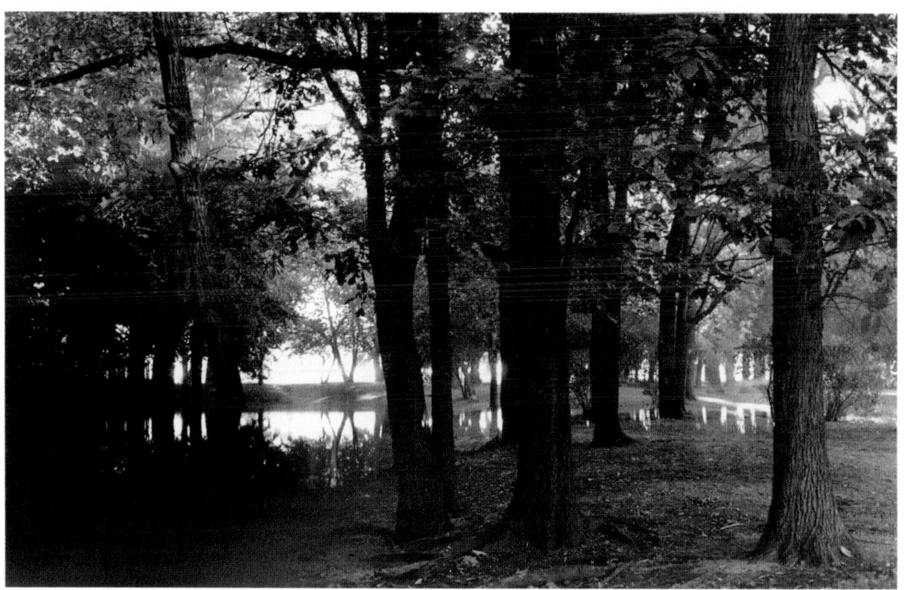

Arturo Herrera. Untitled, 1997. Gelatin silver print. Courtesy of the artist

nor banal, ... caught between the symbolic and the pictorial, an abstract grimace of blazing light and closing darkness"—corresponds to a generalized, almost kitsch forest landscape.[15] By pointing a mirror into the camera's interior, which generated a reflection of the horizon line of the visual field, Herrera captured an image by emphasizing the effects of light and shadow. In addition to evoking Robert Smithson's specular analysis, Herrera's use of the mirror suggests a *mise en abyme,* or a duplication based upon the coexistence of a photograph within a photograph, and with it the reflection of the photograph's infinite reproducibility and the hypothetical potential of this medium to generate an unlimited number of copies and a chain of subsequent reduplications.[16]

The series *Untitled* (2004), comprising eighty gelatin-silver prints, and the digital work *Les Noces* (2007), which pairs projected images from the abovementioned photographic series with an eponymous musical composition by Igor Stravinsky, show Herrera's ambivalent stance in relation to the spectator and the legibility of the image. This ambiguity suggests the exacerbated distance between the society of the spectacle and the conventions of modern painting as an anachronistic and self-contained expression of individual contemplation. However, it is, paradoxically, through the principle of infinite duplication that Herrera recovers the analytical potential of the means of mechanical reproduction to serve as cultural artifacts.[17]

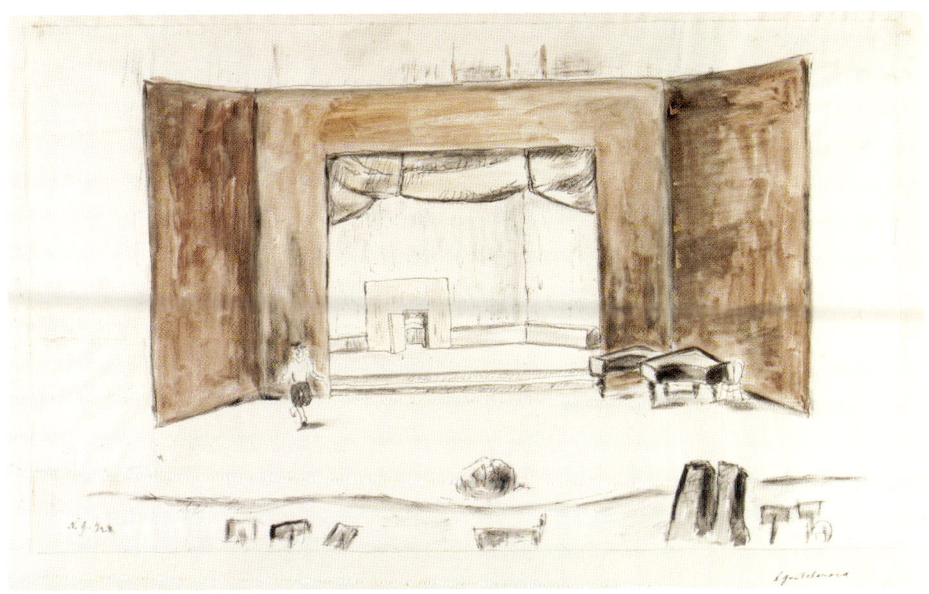

Natalia Goncharova. *Stage-setting design for Scene IV: The Wedding Feast, from the ballet "Les Noces,"* ca. 1923. Pen and ink on paper. V & A Images © 2011 Artists Rights Society (ARS), New York / ADAGP, Paris

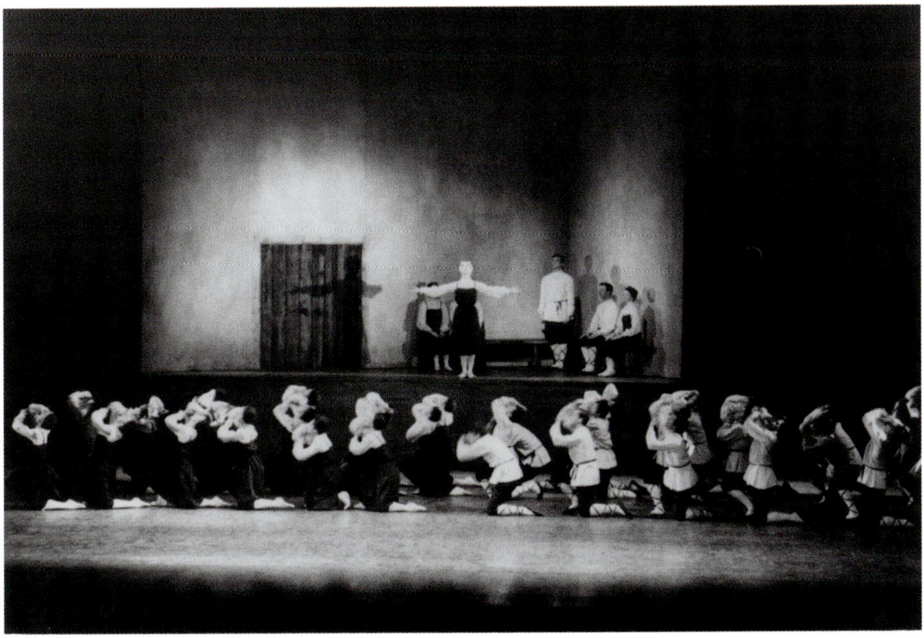

Performance of *Les Noces* at Teatro Colón, Buenos Aires, 1926. Bronislava Nijinska Collection, Music Division, Library of Congress

It was not by accident that the artist came to appropriate Stravinsky's *Les Noces,* which was composed for a ballet of the same name that is widely considered to be one of the few successful *Gesamtkunstwerk* experiments produced by Sergei Diaghilev's Ballet Russes. The music was categorized by some critics as "primitive" for its cryptic and symbolic use of folk culture, and Herrera has used its legacy as a matrix upon which to create a digitally animated photomontage/photocollage. Stravinsky noted the "intransigent" quality of his piece, describing the composition, which he began in 1912, as "perfectly homogenous, impersonal, and mechanical."[18] The score, arranged for solo vocalists, a chorus, four pianos, and percussion, was based on a book of Russian folk songs for peasant weddings. Herrera organized the structure of his work according to the soundtrack of this difficult modern ballet, originally choreographed by Bronislava Nijinska with set design and costumes by the Russian Cubo-Futurist Natalia Goncharova.

In *Les Noces* Herrera does not seek simply to illustrate Stravinsky's arrhythmic composition with his digitized photographs; rather, he uses the score to emphasize the difficulty of constructive a coherent narrative from the eighty abstract and figurative black-and-white images that serve as his source material, and which follow one another in a twenty-seven-minute loop controlled by software that combines them at random and projects them onto two screens. The animated images are made up of drawings and graphic "leftovers" recorded by the artist in his studio, where random elements intervened in the film-development process.[19] The software that controls the loops, which was created by a programmer hired by Herrera, is designed so that the cuts between images are purposefully asynchronous with the beats of the music. This method of stop-gap editing produces a space-time disruption between visuals and sounds, as well as a mechanism of estrangement from the viewer. Moreover, this conceptual approach corresponds to Stravinsky's compositional intentions. Conceived shortly after *The Rite of Spring* (1912), *Les Noces* is structured as a number of cells that produce a pattern of mechanical repetition. Drawing contrasts between the score and the atonal music of Arnold Schoenberg, Theodor Adorno deemed Stravinsky's repetition of motifs and the mechanization of time as destructive and anti-humanist. He criticized Stravinsky for creating a "metric disruption" consistent with the substitution of "expressive time" (which he defined as a metronymic adherence to rhythm) in exchange for the absence of any "expressive subjective fluctuation of the rhythm."[20]

Juxtaposing Stravinsky's arrhythmic composition with his own series of black-and-white photographs, Herrera manages to show the subjective, dramatic, and personal mechanism of the music, which he has transformed into a soundtrack for a digital animation—arguably the most suitable genre for this modern composition. To do so, the artist has masterfully exploited the hybrid nature of the source material, the rhythmic movement of the images (which is, nonetheless, running at its own, arrhythmic pace in relation to the music), the binary structure of the two-channel video presentation, and the transposition of a photo-mechanic image into an electronic one—that is, the move from analog to digital. His interventions aim to suspend the intentionally mechanistic and impersonal nature of Stravinsky's composition, instead eliciting a state of commotion and distraction in the spectator using imagery that is both deeply moving and the spontaneous result of the workings of chance. Furthermore, Stravinsky's use of cells in the composition implied a dialogue between stasis and movement that Herrera expanded through the use of animation.

Neither fiction nor documentary, figuration nor abstraction, animation is a spurious genre that strips bare the binary distinctions of its logic. Herrera further complicates the issue by animating two fields of paired images.[21] As reproductions of fragments of the artist's own works and of his inventory of recycled materials that erode the "analogical perfection" of photography, these images have an indicative quality that refers us back to the heart of the issue examined by Benjamin: the historical adaptation of art to the changes wrought by the technological revolution vis-à-vis the exploration of art's new functions and needs from a technological standpoint. It is against this background that the tensions inherent in the photocollage and photomontage—considered experimental procedures at the beginning of the twentieth century, and which were initially employed in advertising and later in propaganda that embodied the aesthetic, political, and social dilemmas distinguishing the individual from the collective—are played out. Some critics have noted Herrera's resistance to calling his wall paintings murals, a refusal they attribute to his dependence on the logic of modern pictorial conventions.[22] I would argue that Herrera's refusal to use the label is instead due to the political and ideological co-opting of the mural by modernist movements, and to the artist's desire not to restrict a rather complex mode of expression to the parameters prescribed by the dialectical forces of the personal and the collective, the individual and the public.

Walt Disney contributed to the development of a powerful cultural industry by gathering and animating the work of extraordinary illustrators and draftsmen. In the early series known as *Silly Symphonies* (1929–39), Disney animated folk- and fairytales, pushing the boundaries of the cartoon template with a storyline that explored unusual aspects of children's psyches, even the most banal and moralistic.[23] Moreover, the *Silly Symphonies* pioneered the development of a compelling visual narrative through spatial structures that provided a tension with the storytelling (i.e "pumpkin homes that resemble collapsible trailers, tree apartments with leaf welcome mats."[24])

Even if Herrera's recovery of Disney's forgotten heritage is by and large part of a vast archive of images, together with other fragments that are as abstract or representative as an animation, it also recovers the potentialitics of the genre. Using complex and varied archaeological procedures, the artist restates the legacy of modern art and modernist movements as well as the spurious machinery of fragments.

Black and white still from Walt Disney's *Silly Symphony The Merry Dwarfs.* © Disney

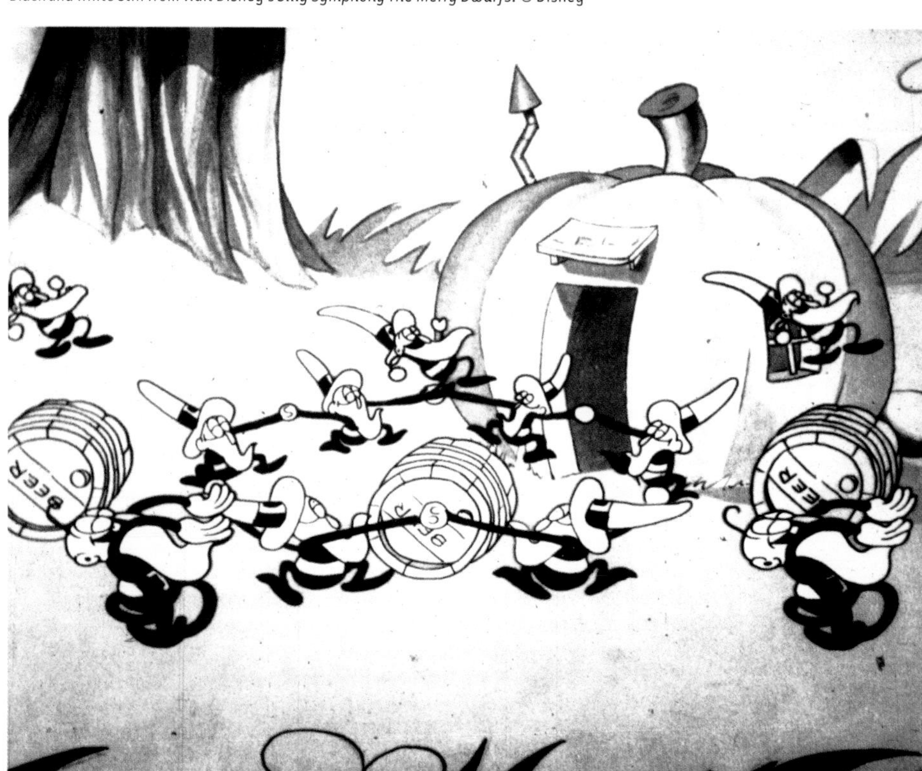

1 See in particular Friedrich Meschede, *Abstracciones híbridas. Comentarios sobre una serie de collages de Arturo Herrera,* in exh. cat., *Arturo Herrera* (Santiago de Compostela: Centro Galego de Arte Contemporáneo, 2005), pp. 27–31; and idem, "Look: On the Collages of Arturo Herrera," in Friedrich Meschede, ed., *Arturo Herrera: You Go First* (New York: D.A.P./Distributed Art Publishers, Inc., 2005) n.p.

2 See Homi K. Bhabba, "DissemiNation: Time, Narrative and the Margins of the Modern Nation," in idem, *Nation and Narration* (London: Routledge, 2006), pp. 312–13.

3 Ralf Christofori, *Arturo Herrera: Photographs* (Torino: Galleria Franco Noero and New York: Sikkema Jenkins & Co., 2004), n.p.

4 Moreover, *Plot* is a heavy steel floor piece that was produced in Germany, which ties the piece in more than one direction to Serra's sculptural practice.

5 With this in mind, the exhaustive jumble and fragmentation of the mass cultural forms and motifs chosen by Herrera in more recent works (for example, *Boy and Dwarf,* 2007) perhaps respond to excessively psychoanalytical interpretations of his work, for which, see Maria Tatar, "Arturo Herrera's Fabulous Monsters," in *Arturo Herrera* (Chicago: Renaissance Society, 1998), pp. 19–24, and Neville Wakefield, "Mix Not Match Not," in ibid., p. 11.

6 Arturo Herrera as interviewed by Josiah McElheny, *Bomb Magazine* 93 (Fall 2005), p. 71.

7 Bhabba, "DissemiNation," p. 312

8 As designated by Tatar, "Arturo Herrera's Fabulous Monsters," pp. 19–24.

9 See Juan Ledezma, "Neither Legible nor Abstract: Arturo Herrera's Work Under the Sign of Ambiguity," in exh. cat., *Arturo Herrera* (Birmingham: Ikon Gallery, 2007), p. 66.

10 T. S. Eliot, "The Dry Salvages," in *Collected Poems, 1909–1962* (New York, San Diego, and London: Harcourt Brace & Company, 1991), p. 194.

11 According to Walter Benjamin, Dada collage "hit the spectator like a bullet, it happened to him, thus acquiring a tactile quality." Walter Benjamin, "The Work of Art in the Age of the Mechanical Reproduction," in John Hanhardt, ed., *Video Culture: A Critical Investigation* (New York: Peregrine Smith Books, 1986), p. 43.

12 Ibid., p. 40.

13 Ibid., p. 43.

14 For Benjamin Buchloh the incorporation of the technical advancements brought about by photography, film, billboards, and other mass modes of agitprop caused a radical paradigm shift within modern art; see Benjamin Buchloh, "From Faktura to Factography," *October* 30 (Autumn 1984), pp. 82–119.

15 Wakefield, "Mix Not Match Not," p. 11

16 Craig Owens examines the deconstructive relationship between reduplication and the specular duplication of photography in his seminal essay "Photography en Abyme," *October* 5 (Summer, 1978), pp. 73–88

17 Perhaps the archaeological treatment that Herrera confers to photography and in a lesser degree to film suggests the anachronistic condition of these modes of expression in the digital era.

18 See Pieter C. van der Toorn, "Stravinsky's Les Noces (Svadebka) and the Prohibition Against Expressive Timing," *The Journal of Musicology* 20, no. 2 (2003), pp. 285–304

19 The film underwent a three- to fourteen-day wash in water before the application of the developing bath, leaving the negative exposed to dust and light.

20 See van der Toorn, "The Prohibition Against Expressive Timing," p. 286

21 A preliminary version of the installation considered four projections.

22 See Ingrid Schaffner, "Cut Up: The Art of Arturo Herrera," in exh. cat., *Arturo Herrera* (Santiago de Compostela: Centro Galego de Arte Contemporánea, 2005), p. 134

23 Walt Disney's *Silly Symphonies* were animated, musical short-feature films based on free adaptations of classic fairytales. The series showcased stories featuring different protagonists and whose story-lines illustrated a sensitivity towards psychological themes relevant to children.

24 Russell Merritt, "Lost on Pleasure Island: Storytelling in Disney's *Silly Symphonies.*" *Film Quarterly* 59, no.1 (Fall 2005), p. 8.

BETWEEN ICONICITY AND ABSTRACTION: THE ERRATIC CONTAMINATION OF A BODY IN PIECES

NUIT BANAI

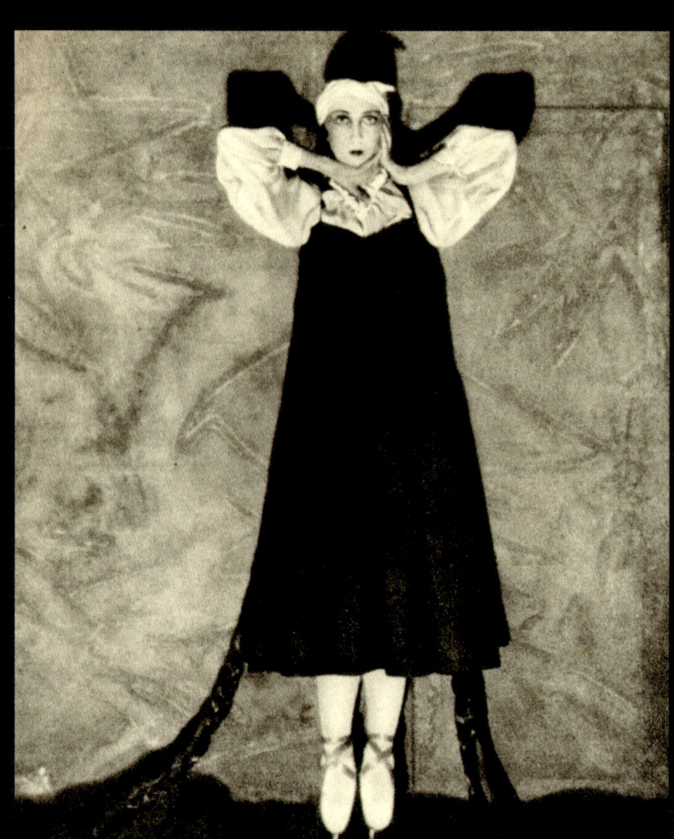

Since the 1990s Arturo Herrera has been excavating the multiple histories of two of the most formative visual paradigms and aesthetic strategies of modernism: collage and abstraction. His appropriation and amalgamation of highly connotative fragments, marks, and traces, procured from avant-garde and mass-cultural image archives of the twentieth century, is a fraught and fragile affair that could all too easily slip into a heroic, pathetic, or nostalgic mode of reception. Yet, Herrera steers clear of such static, singular, and well-rehearsed postures by cultivating supple spaces for generative frictions. In his multimedia practice, the historical, cultural, and ideological points of pressure that came to represent both modernity and modernism are constitutively intertwined with the crisis of our contemporary moment. Although his prolific output of collages, paintings, wall drawings, and installations have raised many important questions, this essay focuses on Herrera's two-channel digital projection *Les Noces* (2007) and its attentiveness to the complicity between visual regimes and the emergence of historically specific subjects and publics. In particular, this essay foregrounds Herrera's negotiation of the fabrication of subjectivity within the globalized networks of the digital age, and the tensions between the carnality of the body and the materiality of vision on the one hand, and the abstraction of the observer's physical and optical armature on the other. Within these critical parameters, some of the following questions come to the fore: How does Herrera's *Les Noces,* with its reiteration and disjunction of divergent stylistic elements, reactivate or reinscribe the spectacular dimensions of Igor Stravinsky's score in relation to our contemporary moment? What kind of body or form of corporeality is posited in this "performance" by a databank of digitized images? Can we infer one or several models of collective identification from the ways in which the installation's computer-generated information stream interacts with the sensory materiality of the body? And what kind of social space is produced by the projection of material artifacts as chance-based movement-images?

Felia Doubrovska as the Bride in the premiere of *Les Noces,* June 13, 1923, Théâtre de la Gaîte-Lyrique, Paris. © Lebrecht Music & Arts

Although the scope of this essay does not allow for a exhaustive exploration of all these avenues, it will suggest that, by orchestrating the chance collision and recombination of semiotic codes, disciplines, technologies, and techniques of visuality, Herrera's *Les Noces* inserts the observer directly into the paths of power that affirm and regulate the experience of becoming a subject. More specifically, in dramatizing the fragmentary and fragmented channels between abstraction and iconicity, through which "experience" is simultaneously produced and consumed, I argue that Herrera carves out a critical space in which to defamiliarize, rearrange, and incorporate the contemporary connectivity between a libidinal economy and the social production of subjects.

LES NOCES: SUBJECTIVE STUTTERING AND SOCIAL FRAGMENTATION

The template for Herrera's exploration is the ballet *Les Noces,* also known as *Svadebka,* or *The Wedding,* one of the most striking collaborations in the history of modernism. In its composite structure and entwinement of multiple ideological and stylistic strands, as well as in the conflicting relationship it establishes between mimesis and abstraction wherein the two are set up as rival epistemological and ontological regimes, *Les Noces* was from its conception a forceful indictment of the naturalization of identity as a stable, singular coordinate. Its early history suggests that the polarity between an economy of similitude and its abstract alterity did strange and "unnatural" things to the libidinal economy of the subject, most notably enforcing an artificial separation between the haptic and the optic, and divorcing the body's epidermis from the chaos of its submerged senses. In its contemporary "revival," *Les Noces* connects with the interlaced and incomplete history of modernism in which a partial, disjointed, and stammering subject emerges from the tensions coursing between iconicity and abstraction.

As suggested by its title, the three-act ballet, scored by Igor Stravinsky, is based on a Russian peasant wedding, but while the music and text are inspired by popular genres and motifs, its spheres of reception were both post-Revolutionary and Western European. This is partially the result of its tumultuous eleven-year gestation, during which the continent experienced the Great War and the Russian Revolution; Sergei Diaghilev encountered financial troubles; Stravinsky toiled through different orchestrations; Natalia Goncharova's designs metamorphosed; and Bronislava Nijinksa's role within the collaboration was not yet solidified. According to Stravinsky, his initial idea, early in 1912, was for a "choral work on the subject of a Russian peasant wedding," and he conceived the title at the same time.[1] Already immersed in *Le Sacre du Printemps* (*The Rite of Spring*), he did not fully turn his attention to the work

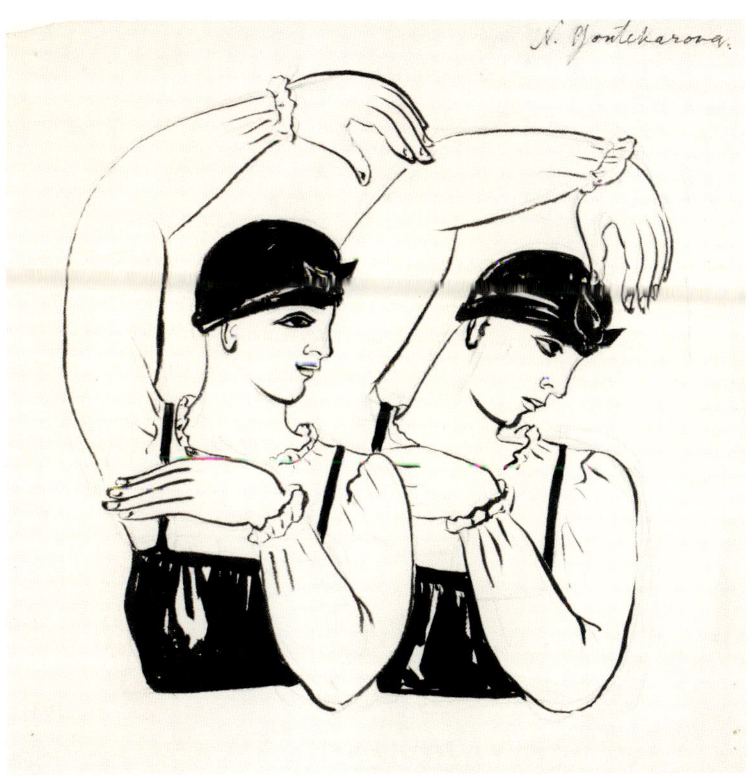

Natalia Goncharova. *Two female dancers (half-length)*. Choreography design for the ballet *Les Noces*, ca. 1923. Pencil, pen, and brush with India ink. V & A Images © 2011 Artists Rights Society (ARS), New York / ADAGP, Paris

until 1914, when he traveled to Russia in search of source material. He found it in a famous ten-volume collection of Russian folk poetry, *Songs Collected by P. V. Kireevsky*, or the *SobranniyePiesni*, published by the Society of Lovers of Russian Literature with the support of Moscow University in 1911.[2] Pyotr Vasilievich Kireevsky, a folklorist and Slavophile, spent many decades in the mid-nineteenth century collecting, with the assistance of collaborators, Russian wedding songs throughout the empire. His ardor for preserving traditional Russian wedding ritual was connected to the Neo-Russian movement's conviction that authentic Russian culture emerged from the indigenous, not the modern, technologically progressive influences imported from the West by Peter the Great. Both Stravinsky and Diaghilev were familiar with the features of the Russian folk style, which inspired the former's composition of *Les Noces* and the latter's mounting of Modest Mussorgsky's *Boris Godunov,* in 1908, and Alexander Borodin's *Prince Igor,* in 1909, for the "Russian Season" in Paris.

Between 1914 and 1923 the ballet mutated numerous times before settling upon its final incarnation. Distancing himself from purely ethnographic ambitions, Stravinsky played freely with his source material, combining different songs and lyrics as the basis for his cantata. The collisions, variations, and permutations in his composition, a leitmotif of his oeuvre, have multiple resonances. While the composer described the "'melodic-rhythmic stutterings' produced by irregularities of accentuation" as a way of capturing the phonetic aspects of the Russian language,[3] he also identified *Les Noces* as, "primarily, the product of the Russian Church."[4] Exiled to Switzerland during World War I and based in France from 1920 to 1939, Stravinsky was also attuned to the stylistic revolutions occurring in modernist literature and cites *Les Noces's* indebtedness to James Joyce's *Ulysses,* "in which the reader seems to be overhearing scraps of conversation without the connecting thread of discourse. ... Both works are trying to *present* rather than to *describe.*"[5] This turning away from description—as a form of mimetic security—might also explain modifications in the musical ensemble, which became more condensed with every variation. Originally conceived for an orchestra of one hundred fifty musicians, the final work contains only four pianos and percussion (xylophone, timpani, crotales, bell, side drums, drums, tambourine, bass drum, cymbals, and triangle). In Stravinsky's words, such a minimal solution "would fulfill [his] conditions. It would be at the same time perfectly homogeneous, perfectly impersonal, and perfectly mechanical."[6] To emphasize these aspects, he also stipulated that "individual roles do not exist in *Les Noces,* but only solo voices that impersonate now one type of character and now another."[7] The composer's choice of words implies that abstraction goes hand in hand with progress, and that it stimulates the liberation of the individual who can now drift from his life of reductive correspondences and, more speculatively, into a new disembodied regime of multiplicity and fantasy. Indeed, some have interpreted the ballet's collaging of folkloric and modernist compositional devices as a political statement about the status of peasant women (and the peasant class as a whole) in pre-revolutionary Russia. Its first staging was seen as an "agitprop" piece that railed against the traditional wedding, with its popular and religious roots, as a symbol of the abstract social forces that govern the individual and the collective.[8] Yet, Stravinsky's embrace of abstraction, approached from a Western perspective, may also articulate a positive ambition to unite the "Russian" with the "technological" and the "cosmopolitan."[9]

The work's multivalent identity, especially its evocation of divergent models of the socius, rests on Goncharova's set and costume designs and Nijinska's choreography. For her part, Goncharova notes that she began to sketch her outfits in 1915 and that they were initially focused on the "festive, folk aspects of weddings ... the colorful costumes and dances that connect weddings with holidays, enjoyment, abundance, and happy vitality."[10] The spare, monochromatic costumes that emerged four versions later articulated Goncharova's more profound understanding of "these marriages of necessity."[11] Made of parachute silk, the costumes resemble work clothes, with the men attired in white shirts and brown trousers and the women in white blouses and brown skirts and scarves. Goncharova noted that the restrained palette would augment Nijinska's vision by allowing the choreographer to "arrange the dances not for distinct characters with a definite role but for identical and, so to speak, interchangeable components."[12] In interviews given more than fifty years after the ballet's premiere, however, Nijinska took credit for the final formulation of the designs, which she considered a vital part of the work's concept.[13]

Diaghilev first approached Nijinska in 1922, after the impresario's first choice, her brother Vaslav Nijinsky, could no longer perform (he suffered a nervous breakdown in 1919 and was later diagnosed with schizophrenia). To avoid the naturalistic "realm of the theater" while aptly communicating the tension between the individual and the collective, Nijinska developed a symbolic set of gestures that drew inspiration from the rituals of the peasant wedding while elevating them to the register of abstraction.[14] At the crux of this vocabulary is the binding of the bride's hair from the single braid of the virgin to the double-braid of the married woman. This ritual, which Stravinsky termed a "religio-sexual custom," is performed by the female phalanx, who dance *en pointe* in small, staccato steps (*pas de bourrée*) in a gesture allusive to "braiding."[15] Nijinska's choreography emphasizes the bride's centrality by drawing on the elongated style of Byzantine icon painting, and she underscores gendered group identification through prostrated, pyramidal, and processional formations, constructing a tension between the bride and groom, the bride and her parents, and, ultimately, the married couple and the community. Although Nijinska wanted the dancers to wear dark blue and beige, evocative of the proletariat, she deferred to Goncharova's neutral color scheme. Despite the lack of explicit ideological references to post-Revolutionary culture, the dance critic André Levinson, who was in exile in Paris at the time, condemned Nijinska for passing "through the collectivist reveries of the Soviets," attacking her for her Marxist choreography: "To this score, so full of vitality and direct power, Mlle Nijinska brought a hollow image of life, mechanical and bloodless. ... [Groups] were arranged in double files, like the soldiers in a firing squad [and transformed into] practicable stage property."[16] This critique was only possible, of course, because *Les Noces* premiered in Paris, billed as a charity event for several Russian expatriate organizations, and it was attended by wealthy members of the Russian émigré community who were sympathetic to Levinson's anti-Soviet point of view.[17]

As for the score, the most severe assessment was offered by Theodor Adorno, who addressed Stravinsky's music in four essays between 1928 and 1961.[18] While it does not single out *Les Noces,* Adorno's critique tackles the principal characteristics of the music and its stylistic shifts over a forty-year period. In "Die stabilisierte Musik" (1928), though not dedicated wholly to Stravinsky, Adorno argues that avant-garde music experienced its truly radical moment before 1914, with the Second Viennese School, and that both neoclassicism and folklorism represented a negative stabilization. Stravinsky, identified with both tendencies, is labeled at once authentic (*Renard,* 1916, and *The Soldier's Tale,* 1918) and reactionary (*Oedipus Rex,* 1927). Four years later, in "Zurgesellschaftlichten Lage der Musik" (1932), Adorno set aside the term "stabilized music" and addressed the differences between "commodity music" and "avant-garde music." While the former participates uncritically in the reification of all spheres of life, the latter recognizes its own complicity through a critical negation of its commodity status. According to the musicologist Max Paddison, Adorno's early writings identify Stravinsky's music as doubly authentic, because it returns to formal styles and types to "reconstitute a lost sense of harmony, totality, and community," and it draws upon fragments from both high and low culture and uses montage techniques to make visible "the fragmentary character of musical material today as well as pointing to social fragmentation."[19]

It was only after the cataclysmic events of World War II—and the publication of his *Dialectics of Enlightenment* (1944)—that Adorno narrowed his definition of what constitutes authenticity. In the seminal book *Philosophy of New Music* (1949), he sets Schönberg's "good" compositions in diametric opposition to Stravinsky's "bad" ones. Based largely on his interpretations of *Petrushka* (1910–11; revised 1947) and *The Rite of Spring* (1913), Adorno charges Stravinsky with embracing the regressive power of myth and archaism and contributing to the disintegration of the bourgeois model of subjectivity. Alluding to *Les Noces,* Adorno writes, "the works between *Sacre* and the turn to neo-classicism imitate the gesture of regression, as it belongs to the dissolution of individual identity. Through this attitude, these works would appear to achieve collective authenticity." However, "the search for musical equivalents of the 'collective unconscious' prepares the transition to the installation of a regressive collective

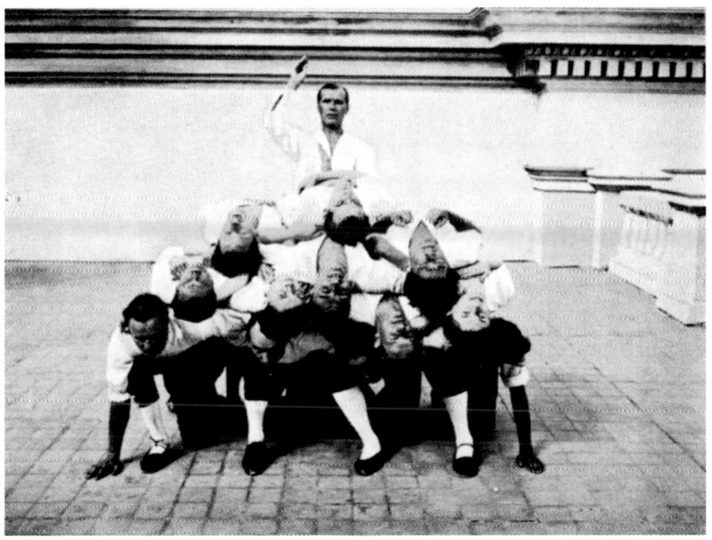

Rehearsal of *Les Noces* on the roof of the Théâtre de Monte-Carlo, 1923. Bronislava Nijinska Collection, Music Division, Library of Congress

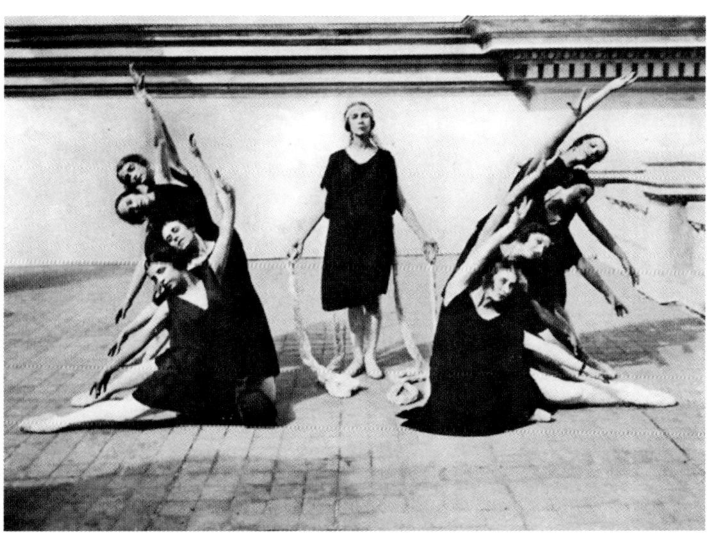

Rehearsal of *Les Noces* on the roof of the Théâtre de Monte-Carlo, 1923. Bronislava Nijinska Collection, Music Division, Library of Congress

as a positive accomplishment."[20] Continuing in this vein in his final critique, "Stravinsky: A Dialectical Portrait" (1961), the philosopher contended that Stravinsky's nondevelopmental temporal succession mimics the structure of myth. "As a temporal art," he writes, "music is bound to the fact of succession and is hence as irreversible as time itself. By starting, it commits itself to carrying on, to becoming something new, to developing."[21] If a developmental dynamic is the only possible means to criticality, then Stravinsky's music, with its emphasis on repetition and permutation, can only be regarded as reactionary in Adorno's estimation. Although treated only summarily here, Adorno's analysis of Stravinsky raises significant questions about the role of aesthetic production in shaping the experience of life in an advanced capitalist economy. Indeed, Adorno's delineation of the intertwinement between repetition and fragmentation as constituents of subjective and collective formations within the historical condition of modernity remains a central interpretive mechanism. Yet, it is simply insufficient to graft Adorno's formal, moral, and ideological precepts onto Herrera's work as if its current moment of projection and reception is inconsequential.

REPETITION AND FRAGMENTATION: THE ABSTRACTED BODY IN THE CAPITALIST SOCIUS

Repetition and fragmentation are indelibly woven into both the tissue of the capitalist socius and Herrera's *Les Noces.* Through a set of formal decisions, however, the artist makes visible the impossibility of maintaining negative dialectics as a critical strategy through which to negotiate the intensified, delirious processes of contemporary experience-production.[22] In this regard it is crucial that Herrera chose to omit the centralized stage as a focal point and to avoid replicating Diaghilev's dancers, Goncharova's costumes, and Nijinska's choreography. If the original production already condemned mimesis as an antiquated visual system, Herrera's decision to eschew a mimetic reproduction of the original performance adds an additional layer of distantiation. As we shall see, the power of the copy is evoked as a wistful and somewhat mutilated vestige at the same time that it is complicated by the decentralized productive forces that have superseded it in the digital age.

Transforming the immersed spectator into a phenomenological conduit between two flat interfaces within a three-dimensional chamber underscores the translation of the original *Les Noces* into a contemporary manifestation. In this theater, eighty black-and-white photographic images culled from Herrera's oeuvre are animated on two screens (each divided into two subscreens) on opposite sides of the darkened gallery. With each loop of Stravinsky's score, specially designed computer software accesses a database and randomly chooses images in relation to the music's pitch. At any given moment during the twenty-seven-minute "performance," four discrete images "dance" arbitrarily on the two screens. They are composed of closely cropped abstract fragments and collaged elements that appear as so many cavorting smears, squiggles, drips, surfaces, and filaments. Every so often, an identifiable character or part-object from Herrera's lexicon appears in the mix: a Disney dwarf or a faintly silhouetted toy duck. The labor intensive fabrication of this image archive, which has occupied Herrera for approximately twenty years, is at once directed by and open to chance operations. Herrera's process begins with the collection of source material: thousands of scraps of paper culled from magazines, newspapers, and illustrated books. Slicing into these "originals" to make variously shaped and sized snippets, he painstakingly builds multilayered collages occasionally embellished with poster paints, watercolors, or colored cardboard. This jumble of deracinated indices is then photographed, often at close range, so that the initial act of hand-cutting the paper is amplified by the lenticular incision that zooms in and reframes discrete elements of the collaged composition. The sealed rolls of film are then submerged in water for varying lengths of time, absorbing liquid and further abstracting the indexical marks that slip further from referential reach.

These operative cuts, both violent and tender, through which Herrera's archive is built deface the notion of mimetic coherence. And, indeed, as the anthropologist Michael Taussig has so eloquently argued, "the cut of de/facement ... works on objects the way jokes work on language, bringing out their inherent magic nowhere more than when those objects have become routinized and social, like money or the nation's flag where God has long been put in his place."[23] Using scissors and the camera's mechanical lens to cut, fragment, and slice into the idiom of collage and abstraction, Herrera defaces the ways in which modernism has buried the libidinal economy of the body and made it the most "public secret" of the twentieth century. In other words, defacement functions as an alternative kind of critique by releasing "the (sacred) surplus" that makes visible "that which is generally known but cannot be articulated."[24] What is revealed in this mixed archive is both the contemporary memory of a historical body and a proposal for a new model of embodiment. As the music swells and wanes and the voices boom and falter, the images pulsate like a virtual corps de ballet, responding to and "personifying" the technological code of the performance-event. Disavowing mimesis at every turn while making visible its submerged excesses, these images should not be conceived as substitutes for the dancers. Although traces of the performers are evoked in absentia, the shimmering images are contemporary manifestations of our own carnal infrastructure and its intertwinement

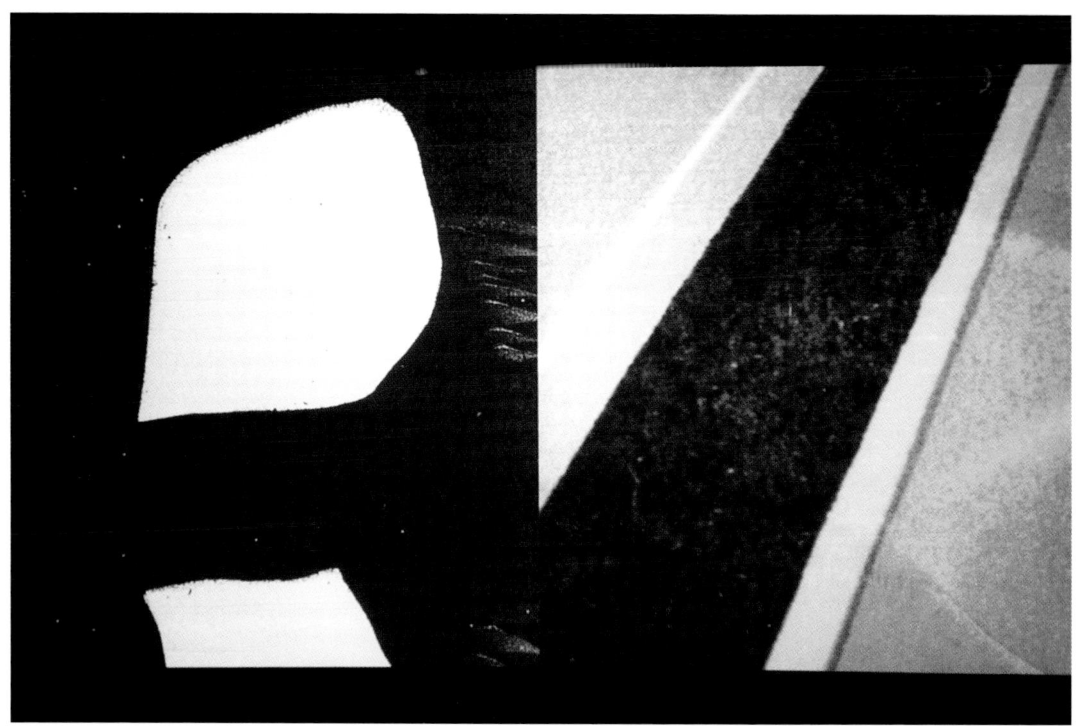

Stills from Arturo Herrera's digital projection *Les Noces*, 2007. Photograph by Arturo Sánchez

with a fragmented, abstracted flow of media. Within this theater, the "protagonists" are the technological and social forces of abstraction that give rise to Herrera's artistic vocabulary and that inscribe and transform the spectator into both a surface and an environment for the production and projection of a social body.

Herrera thus intensifies the image of the individual and of the public body as visualized by Stravinsky, Goncharova, and Nijinska circa 1923. If it ever existed, the monolithic rigidity between the dialectical poles inscribed within the regimes of iconicity and abstraction—"organic" versus "mechanistic" and "traditional" versus "progressive"—definitively collapses. The artist urges such a dissolution by the work's double address, which situates the viewer in an "objective" relationship vis-à-vis the aesthetic experience while simultaneously plunging him or her within the body's inner membrane and the messy, irrational flow of its libidinal economy. Thus, the frontal and symmetrical monumentality of the screens suggests a phenomenological coherence, while their fracture into two and four makes it impossible to be in the full "presence" of either a unified optical and physical event or an integral sense of self. This dynamic between integrity and dissolution is also evident in the artist's choice of techniques, particularly the elision between abstraction and collage as a simultaneous dematerialization and concretization of the body. By choosing these two modernist paradigms, Herrera evinces the crisis of representation that erupted in the visual arts in the first two decades of the twentieth century. In this fertile moment, he reminds us, abstraction repealed the authority of mimetic naturalism, while collage disrupted the analogous quality of the painted surface. As argued forcefully by Rosalind Krauss, while the idea of representation was being radically rethought via transformations in figure/ground relationships in both abstraction and collage, the figure never really disappeared.[25] Rather, it went "underground," where it persistently contaminated the transcendental purity of the modernist mandate. In Herrera's *Les Noces,* then, the body is implicit even in its apparent absence. More than just a body-on-display, however, it is a body-turned-inside-out, with both its physical and psychological armature lacerated and laid bare to reveal a volatile nervous system linked to a constellation of political, economic, and technological forces. This, at least, is the sense one gets from the bifurcated installation, which erodes stable boundaries and suggests the precariousness and contingency of subjective incorporation. In my interpretation, the succession of grainy contours, shapes, and silhouettes that shimmy and flicker across the split screens do not only interject themselves into our sensory continuum but emerge from it, too. *Les Noces* imagines what it would be like to shed the body's protective skin—and the hygienic veneer of modernism—and witness the impressions and impregnations that constitute its various archives.

In 1967 Raoul Vaneigem wrote that "the concepts and abstractions which rule us have to be returned to their source, to lived experience. ... The sole authority is one's lived experience; and this everyone must prove to be everyone else's."[26] Although Vaneigem was speaking of ways to repossess co-opted urban space through direct physical intervention in the context of the Long Sixties in France, his words may help elucidate the way in which Herrera's *Les Noces* operates today as a more muted intercession. Disengaging from the revolutionary rhetoric of both the Russian avant-garde and the Situationist International, the artist seeks subtle ways to engage with the collision between visual regimes and the political sphere. If we agree that the work maintains musical allusions to the Russian peasant wedding, put forth as a brutal rite of passage, but transforms them into an abstract choreography of bodily intertwinement and a theater of libidinal forces, might we, then, approach this strategic disequilibrium of physical and perceptual limits, which leaves the spectator submitting to multiple vectors, as a politics of sorts? Indeed, with the spectator posited as both an interface and a performance, what emerges in this work is the problem of aesthetic and subjective reinvention via the collision between modernism (as a multivalent body of knowledge) and a contemporary spectator (constituted by increasingly abstract visual technologies and processes of socialization that penetrate and reconfigure their corporeal density). Even as *Les Noces* produces new heterogeneous connotations and connections through its variable pacing, imagistic multiplicity, and spectatorial fragmentation, it would be remiss not to speculate whether it also fabricates manageable subjects by objectifying perceptual and physical experience through the pathways of abstraction. Indeed, inserted as a conduit, the body is harnessed toward different effects of power on the level of the libidinal and the somatic. In this hallucinatory link between figure and ground, Herrera's inventory of images projects a spectator who is simultaneously endowed with creative freedom and rife for administration. This dancing specter—part-collage, part-abstraction—emerges from the marriage between Herrera's predominantly chance-based practice and the software that is programmed to deliver an infinite sequencing of chance. Through the installation's mixed fabrication and nuanced historical and conceptual textures, one's "lived experience," to return to Vaneigem's decree, contains the paradoxical potential for both arbitrary and highly mediated forms of becoming. Hinged at this productive threshold, *Les Noces's* erratic contamination of communicative and visual rationality suggests that the contours of subjective and social space might be unraveled and rewoven with every image and within each body.

I wish to thank Gabriela Rangel and Arturo Herrera for their gracious invitation to contribute to the catalogue, Michael Jenkins for generously providing me with important material on Herrera's previous work, and Taylor McVay for her invaluable research assistance.

1 Igor Stravinsky and Robert Craft, *Expositions and Developments* (London: Faber and Faber, 1962), p. 114. The scholar Arthur Comegno dates Stravinsky's conception of the work to 1913, when he first mentions the ballet in a correspondence; see *Dance Research Journal* 18, no. 2, "Russian Folklore Abroad" (Winter 1986–87), p. 31.

2 For a comprehensive history of the Kireevsky Collection, see Roberta Reeder, "The Kireevsky Collection and the Neo-Russian Movement," in *Dance Research Journal* 18, no. 2, "Russian Folklore Abroad" (Winter 1986–87), pp. 32–36.

3 The composer is quoted in Mikhail Druskin, *Igor Stravinsky: His Life, Works and Views,* trans. Martin Cooper (Cambridge: Cambridge University Press, 1983), p. 53.

4 The complete quote can be found in Sally Banes, *Dancing Women: Female Bodies on Stage* (London: Routledge, 1998), p. 108.

5 Stravinsky's reference to James Joyce appears in Robert Johnson, "Ritual and Abstraction in Nijinksa's *Les Noces," Dance Chronicle* 10, no. 2 (1987), p.148

6 Stravinsky describes the evolution of the piece in Kenneth Gloag, "Russian Rites: *Petrushka, The Rite of Spring,* and *Les Noces,"* in Jonathan Cross, ed., *The Cambridge Companion to Stravinsky* (Cambridge: Cambridge University Press, 2003), p. 95.

7 Stravinsky and Craft, *Expositions and Developments,* p. 115.

8 Sally Banes discusses the social and political status of peasant women in Russia and the patriarchal character of marriage laws prior to the Revolution of 1917. She characterizes *Les Noces* as "the most accurate in describing women's real-life situations," and interprets it as an instance of agitprop. She notes, however, that it does not offer a solution to the issue like other agitprop theater pieces of the time; see *Dancing Women,* pp. 108–22.

9 Drue Fergison, "Bringing *Les Noces* to the Stage," in Lynn Garafola and Nancy Van Norman Baer, eds., *The Ballets Russes and Its World* (New Haven: Yale University Press, 1999), p. 170.

10 Natalia Goncharova, "The Metamorphoses of the Ballet 'Les Noces,'" *Leonardo* 12, no. 2 (Spring 1979), p. 137.

11 Ibid, p. 140.

12 Quoted in Alexander Schouvaloff, *The Art of Ballets Russes* (New Haven and London: Yale University Press, 1997), p. 208. Goncharova spoke about her designs with A.-G. d'E, "Mme Gontcharova nous parle du décor et des costumes de 'Noces,' Les Ballets Russes," *Le Parisien* (June 14, 1923).

13 Bronislava Nijinska, "Creation of 'Les Noces,'" trans. and introd. Jean Serafetinides and Irina Nijinska, *Dance Magazine* (December 1974), p. 59.

14 Quoted in Banes, *Dancing Women,* p. 111.

15 Ibid, p. 112.

16 André Levison's critique of Nijinska's choreography is quoted in Lynn Garafola, *Legacies of Twentieth-Century Dance* (Middletown, Conn.: Wesleyan University Press, 2005), p.130.

17 The scant information on the ballet's premiere is provided in Fergison, "Bringing *Les Noces* to the Stage," p. 183.

18 Max Paddison, "Stravinsky as Devil: Adorno's Three Critiques," in Cross, *The Cambridge Companion to Stravinsky,* pp. 192–202.

19 Ibid, p. 195.

20 Theodor W. Adorno, "Stravinsky and Restoration," in *Philosophy of Modern Music* (New York: The Seabury Press, 1973), p. 162.

21 Idem, "Stravinsky: A Dialectical Portrait," in *Quasi una fantasia,* trans. Rodney Livingstone (London: Verso, 1992), p. 147.

22 Adorno's evaluation of Stravinsky and his criteria for aesthetic judgment, especially the espousal of negative dialectics, have not been immune to censure; see Carl Dahlaus, "Das Problem der 'höherenKritik': Adorns PolemikgegenStrawinsky," *Neue Zeitschrift für Musik* 148, no. 5 (1987), pp. 9–15; Peter Bürger, "The Decline of the Modern Age," trans. David J. Parent, *Telos* 62 (Winter 1984–85), pp. 117–30; and Jean-François Lyotard, "Adorno as the Devil" [1973], trans. Robert Hurley, *Telos* 19 (1974–75), pp. 127–37.

23 Michael Taussig, *Defacement: Public Secrecy and the Labor of the Negative* (Stanford: Stanford University Press, 1999), pp. 3–5.

24 Ibid, p. 3.

25 Rosalind E. Krauss, *The Optical Unconscious* (Cambridge, Mass.: MIT Press, 1994); and *The Picasso Papers* (Cambridge, Mass.: MIT Press, 1999).

26 Raoul Vaneigem, *Traité de savoir-vivre à l'usage des jeunes generations* (Paris: Éditions Gallimard, 1967), p. 253. The complete passage reads, "*Les abstractions, les notions qui nous dirigent, il convient désormais de les ramener à leur source, à l'expérience vécue, non pour les justifier, mais pour les corriger au contraire, pour les inverser, les rendre au vécu dont elles sont issues et dont elles n'auraient jamais dû sortir! C'est à cette condition que les homes reconnaîtront sous peu que leur créativité individuelle ne se distingue pas de la créativité universelle. Il n'y a pas d'autorité en dehors de ma propre expérience vécue; c'est ce que chacun doit prouver à tous.*"

ABSTRACTION AND THE DANCE: BRONISLAVA NIJINSKA'S *LES NOCES*

LYNN GARAFOLA

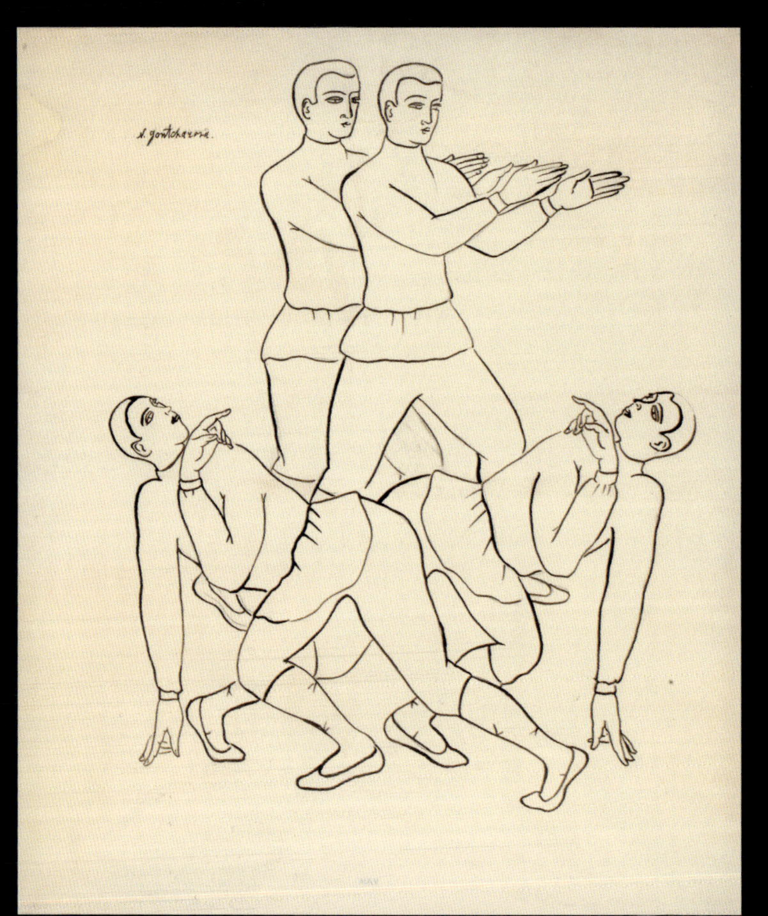

On June 13, 1923, at the Théatre de la Gaité-Lyrique in Paris, the ballet company of Serge Diaghilev gave the first performance of *Les Noces.* Interest ran high in the new work, which depicted a peasant wedding in old Russia, and in the trio of Russian artists who created it. The score, by Igor Stravinsky, was ten years in the making and rumored to be a masterpiece; the scenery and costumes were by Natalia Goncharova, a painter celebrated for her brilliant palette and stylized treatment of folk material. The choreography was by Bronislava Nijinska, who was just beginning to make a name for herself as a choreographer, although she was already familiar to audiences as a dancer. A charter member of the Ballets Russes—or "Russian Ballet"—as Diaghilev's company was called, Nijinska had spent the years of World War I and the early Revolutionary period in Moscow and Kiev. There, under the influence of avant-garde painters and theater directors, she had remade herself as an innovative, experimental artist and created her first abstract works. *Les Noces,* a work of radical formalism permeated with the euphoria of the first Revolutionary years, represented the culmination of that process. *Les Noces* sealed Nijinska's reputation as a creative artist of outstanding importance and secured her a place in the great, overwhelmingly male tradition of ballet choreography.

Unlike most ballets conceived and presented by the Ballets Russes, *Les Noces* was dominated by its choreographer, although this was not the case at first. Stravinsky had conceived the work as a companion piece to *The Rite of Spring,* but in the decade that followed, it changed dramatically, shedding its full orchestra and exotic instruments for a spartan combination of piano, percussion, and voice—a process that reflected Stravinsky's transformation from a Russian nationalist composer to a Western neoclassical one. Goncharova, who joined the project early on, followed Stravinsky's lead, gradually simplifying her designs but stopping short of the functionalism they would ultimately achieve. Choreographers, meanwhile, came and went. For years the project remained in limbo.

In 1922 Nijinska came on the scene. She had rejoined the Ballets Russes in 1921 and given proof of her choreographic gifts while trying, unsuccessfully, to interest Diaghilev in projects

Natalia Goncharova. *A Group of Male Dancers.* Design for costumes and choreography for the ballet *Les Noces,* ca. 1923. Pencil, pen, and brush with India ink. V & A Images © 2011 Artists Rights Society (ARS), New York / ADAGP, Paris

she had conceived in Soviet Russia. Now Diaghilev offered her a plum assignment—*Les Noces.* In a memoir written in the 1960s, she recalled her thrill at hearing Stravinsky play the score for the first time, and her disappointment at seeing Goncharova's "sumptuously Russian" designs. Boldly, she announced to "Sergei Pavlovich" that they were all wrong, both for Stravinsky's music, with its "disturbing" rhythms and deeply Russian character, and for her conception of the choreography.[1] In a huff, Diaghilev dropped the project.

One year later, his interest in it revived. In one of his early meetings with Nijinska, she seized a pencil, sketching as she explained her ideas for the setting and choreography. The boldness of her vision excited him, her insistence on rejecting props, pantomime, and what she called "Russo-Boyar" color. She wanted simple costumes; she wanted everyone dressed the same and scenery that served as a neutral backdrop to the dancing. Won over by her ideas, Diaghilev gave Nijinska a free hand, allowing her to stamp her artistic vision on the entire production. For the first and only time, he allowed the choreographer of one of his works to function as its producer.

The history of ballet is full of weddings but none that remotely resembles Nijinska's. *Les Noces* comprises four tableaux—the Blessing of the Bride, the Blessing of the Groom, the Departure of the Bride, and the Wedding Feast—performed without a musical break. There is no narrative to speak of, no colorful peasants, religious ceremonies, mating dances, or Prince Charming—only a bride, a groom, a mother who laments the loss of her daughter, and a mirthless community inebriated by Stravinsky's driving rhythms. In his music Nijinska heard the gendered tragedy of old Russia, the sacrifice of its daughters, the forced marriage of its children, and, above all, the pain of the young girl as she contemplated her future. "I saw a dramatic quality in the fate of the bride and groom," she wrote in a reminiscence long after the ballet's premiere:

> **The young girl knows nothing ... about her future family nor what lies in store for her. Not only will she be subject to her husband, but also to his parents. It is possible that after being loved and cherished by her own kin, she may be nothing more, in her new, rough family, than a useful extra worker, just another pair of hands. The soul of the innocent is in disarray—she is bidding good-bye to her carefree youth and to her loving mother. For his part, the young groom cannot imagine what life will bring close to this young girl, whom he scarcely knows, if at all. How can such souls rejoice during their wedding ceremonies? ... From the very beginning I had this vision of *Les Noces.*[2]**

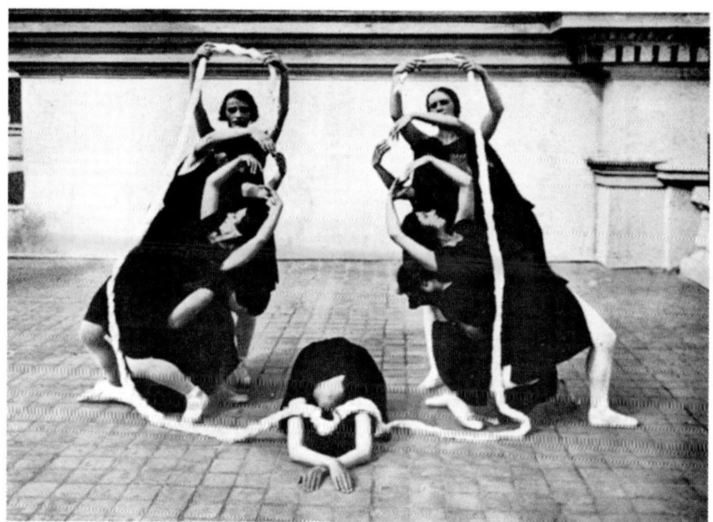

Rehearsal of *Les Noces* on the roof of the Théâtre de Monte-Carlo, 1923. Bronislava Nijinska Collection, Music Division, Library of Congress

Nijinska's vision was a powerful response to Stravinsky's music but not to his work as a whole. Except for the section titles, she ignored the composer's libretto, including the ode to connubial love that brings the work to an ecstatic end. This was in keeping with her dictum that "there should be no 'librettism' in theater," as she wrote in her diary in 1921, and her view, articulated in her sprawling treatise of 1918, that choreography, like contemporary painting, should aspire to the condition of pure form and should privilege the artist's "creativity and expression."[3] In Kiev she had already choreographed at least two abstract works, and with *Les Noces* she picked up where she had left off, transforming the libretto into what she described as a "hidden theme for a pure choreography." She called the work a "choreographic concerto,"[4] adopting a musical term (one of many that she would apply to her work) to underscore the fundamentally abstract nature of the stage action.

As an art of the human body, dance can never be fully abstract. However, as Nijinska demonstrated in *Les Noces,* both the architecture of a dance work and its choreography can be treated abstractly. Her transformation of the libretto is one manifestation of this tendency; another is her insistence on plain, uniform costuming, an abstraction in brown and white of everyday peasant dress. She treats ballet language in a similarly abstract manner, simplifying it and stripping it of the niceties of traditional classical style. Ballet women spend years developing soft, expressive arms, airy jumps, pliant feet, and harmonious lines. In *Les Noces* one sees their converse: tubular arms that end in fists; pointes that stab the ground like screams; leaden jumps; steps performed with the rhythmic insistence of a machine. With the blank faces of Orthodox icons, the Bride's attendants swaddle her neck in ten-foot-long braids, then plait themselves into a tress of living bodies—the first of Nijinska's remarkable architectural constructions.

If the women's choreography in *Les Noces* rests on transformed classical movements, that for the men draws on Russian folk dance. Here, again, Nijinska simplifies familiar movement, exposing its "bones" and stripping it of personal expression. She shows us the abstract geometry of barrel jumps and squat steps, and the possibility of fresh combinations once the old grammatical rules are tossed out. In a manner similar to Stravinsky's approach to the music, Nijinska builds her choreography from repeated units of movement, "cells" that replicate one

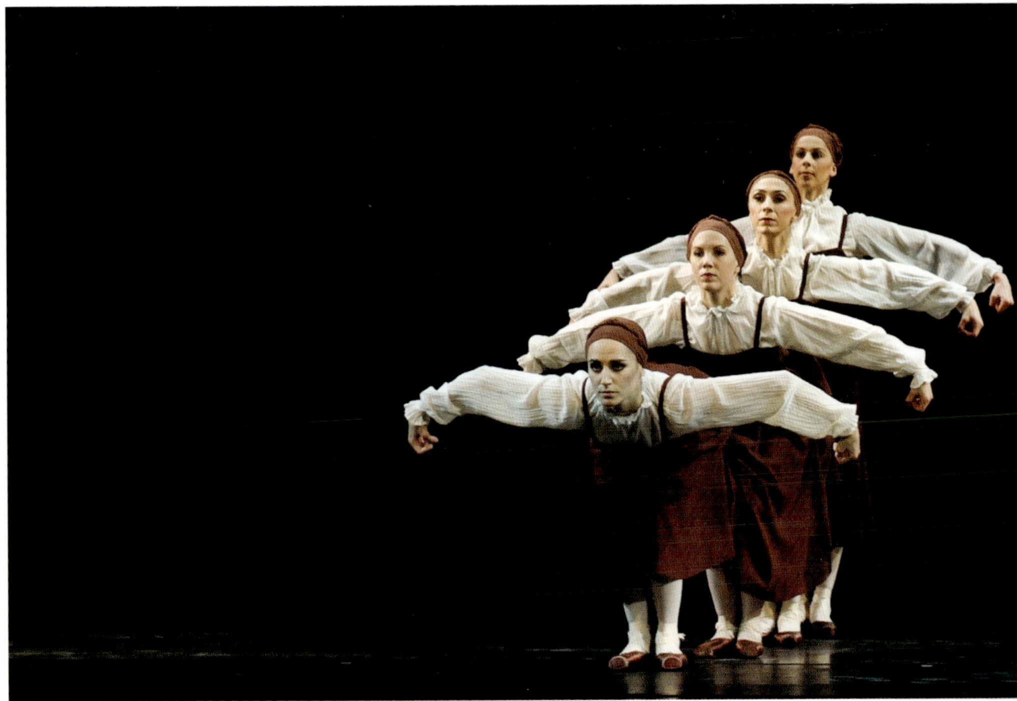

another with mechanical precision. No wonder dancers who have performed *Les Noces* speak of learning the choreography as a feat of memory and, years after the experience, still remember the complicated counts.

In one of several abrasive reviews of the ballet, André Levinson referred to Nijinska's choreography as "Marxist."[5] Specifically, he accused her of slighting the individual for the mass: in "swallowing" the dancer, he wrote, she had "leveled" his art. *Les Noces,* in fact, was predicated on the very absence of the individual. The Bride and the Groom, and their respective sets of parents, exert no control over their destiny; they are victims of a higher power. Within the universe of the ballet, design is fate: architecture spells out the theme of social determinism. Nijinska masses her ensemble into human pyramids, phalanxes, mounds, and wedges—a spatial architecture that transposed to dance the nonobjective forms of Constructivism. Such forms abound in Nijinska's notebooks and diagrams of the period.[6] Worked on graph paper,

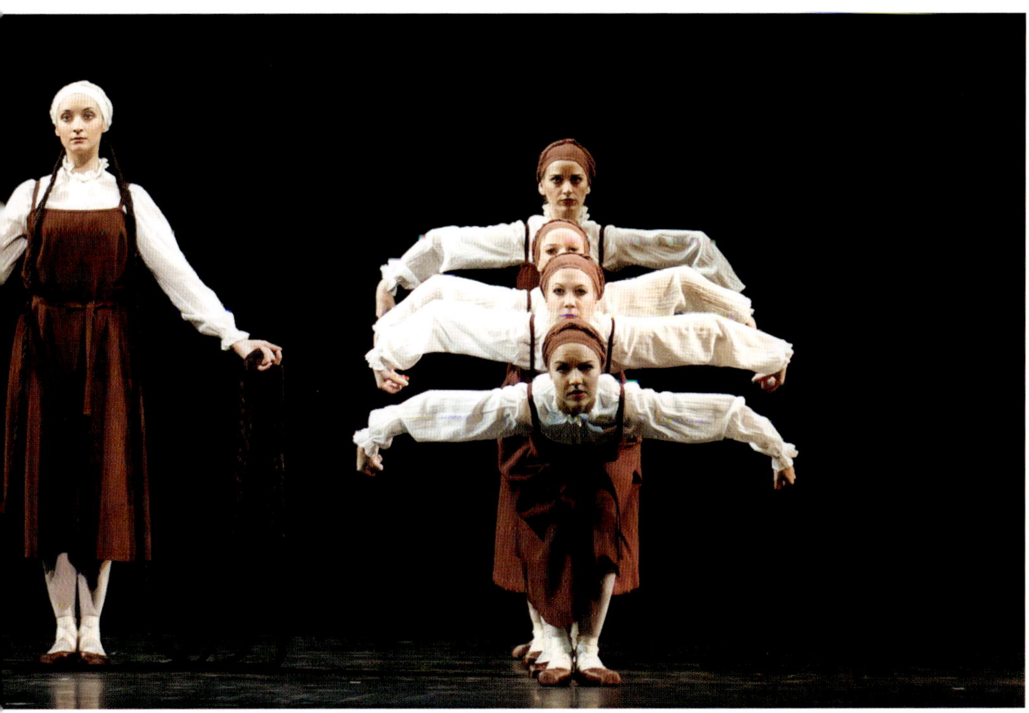

Scene I: Consecration of the Bride, from the ballet *Les Noces,* performed at the Royal Ballet, London, 2004. Photograph by Bill Cooper

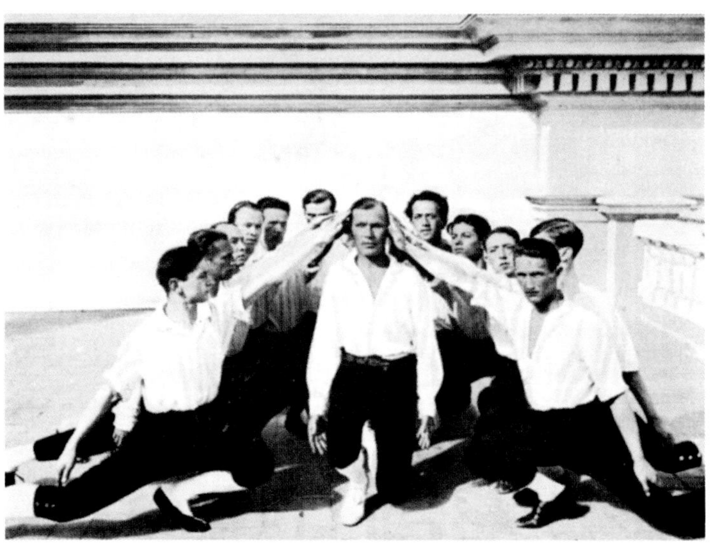

Rehearsal of *Les Noces* on the roof of the Théâtre de Monte-Carlo, 1923. Bronislava Nijinska Collection, Music Division, Library of Congress

the diagrams are totally geometric, as if the space of the stage, represented by an enclosing square, encompassed only abstract forms. Often the latter are circular figures—quadrants, arcs, loops, spheres—while at other times they take a linear form: wedges, triangles, and squares that seem to come straight from the canvases of Malevich, Tatlin, or Exter. Several of these forms reappear in the human massings of *Les Noces.*

Les Noces is a work that belongs fully to the ensemble. The Bride and Groom are little more than ciphers, their fate determined by others. The parents, too, have little voice; even a mother's tears change nothing. Rather, Nijinska saw the action of the ballet as propelled by collective entities: the Bride and her attendants, the Groom and his attendants, and, finally, in the culminating tableau, the Wedding Feast, the full cast of the ballet, divided into male and female "blocs." Here, Nijinska wrote, "all the action would be choreographically delivered by the 'power' of the whole mass of the ensemble."[7] Nijinska's choice of language—above all her use of such politically charged words as "mass" and "bloc"—reveal her debt to the radical ideas of Kiev-based theater directors such as Les Kurbas and Marko Tereshchenko, both of whom made rhythmic gesture and corporeal expression key features of their work. Tereshchenko, in particular, emphasized mass movement in his productions, denying the importance of the playwright, director, and actor as individuals while eliminating scenery and even dialogue to create "a theater of collective art."[8] Nijinska taught classes at his experimental studio, the All-Ukrainian Central Studio Drama Group, and from her notes it appears that they served together on official bodies relating to the arts.[9] Even if she maintained a discreet silence about her relationship with the new Soviet state once she emigrated to the West, *Les Noces* testified to the impact of ideas generated by some of the regime's most radical artists.

Nijinska used abstraction to inflect the ballet with a personal sensibility; that it was a woman's sensibility seems obvious from both the choreography and her writing about the ballet. *Les Noces* spoke to women in a way different than it did to men. It created a space in which the female voice could be heard and the expression of female subjectivity could take form, in male as well as female bodies. Hers was the voice of a woman whose personal discontents deeply affected her view of marriage: Nijinska's husband had more than once abandoned her for other women, leaving her, finally, with two young children and an aging mother to support. The pessimism with which she viewed heterosexual relations, to say nothing of marriage, suggests that something akin to a feminist consciousness was at work in the ballet. It was abstraction that allowed Nijinska to express choreographically that which had to be said—but could only be said without words.

1 Bronislava Nijinska, "Creation of 'Les Noces,'" trans. and introd. Jean Serafetinides and Irina Nijinska, *Dance Magazine* (December 1974), p. 60.

2 Ibid.

3 Bronislava Nijinska, "Diary 1919–1922," entry for 14 March 1921, Box 59, Folder 1; "School and Theater of Movement 1918," Box 55, Folder 5, p. 2, Bronislava Nijinska Collection, Music Division, Library of Congress (hereafter BNC).

4 Bronislava Nijinska, "Reflections About the Production of *Les Biches* and *Hamlet* in Markova-Dolin Ballets," trans. Lydia Lopokova, *The Dancing Times* (February 1937), p. 618.

5 André Levinson, "La Danse: Où sont les 'Ballets russes,'" *Comoedia* (18 June 1923), p. 4.

6 See, for example, the diagrams in Box 48, Folder 8, BNC.

7 Nijinska, "Creation of 'Les Noces,'" p. 60.

8 For Kurbas, see Virlana Tkacz, "Towards a New Vision of Theatre: Les Kurbas's Work at the Young Theatre in Kyiv" and "Les Kurbas's Early Work at the Berezil: From Bodies in Motion to Performing the Invisible" in Irena R. Makaryk and Virlana Tkacz, eds., *Modernism in Kyiv: Jubilant Experimentation* (Toronto: University of Toronto Press, 2010), pp. 278–309 and 362–85. For Tereshchenko, see Hanna Veselovska, "Kyiv's Multicultural Theatrical Life, 1917–1926," in *Modernism in Kyiv*, pp. 260–64, and the entry on the "Mykhailychenko Theater" in the Encyclopedia of Ukraine, vol. 3 (1993).

9 Nijinska mentions him in her outline for an autobiographical volume covering the years 1914–34, Box 34, Folder 18, and in her Kiev name lists, Box 66, Folder 5, BNC.

INTERVIEW
ARTURO HERRERA WITH DAME MONICA MASON AND CHRISTOPHER NEWTON

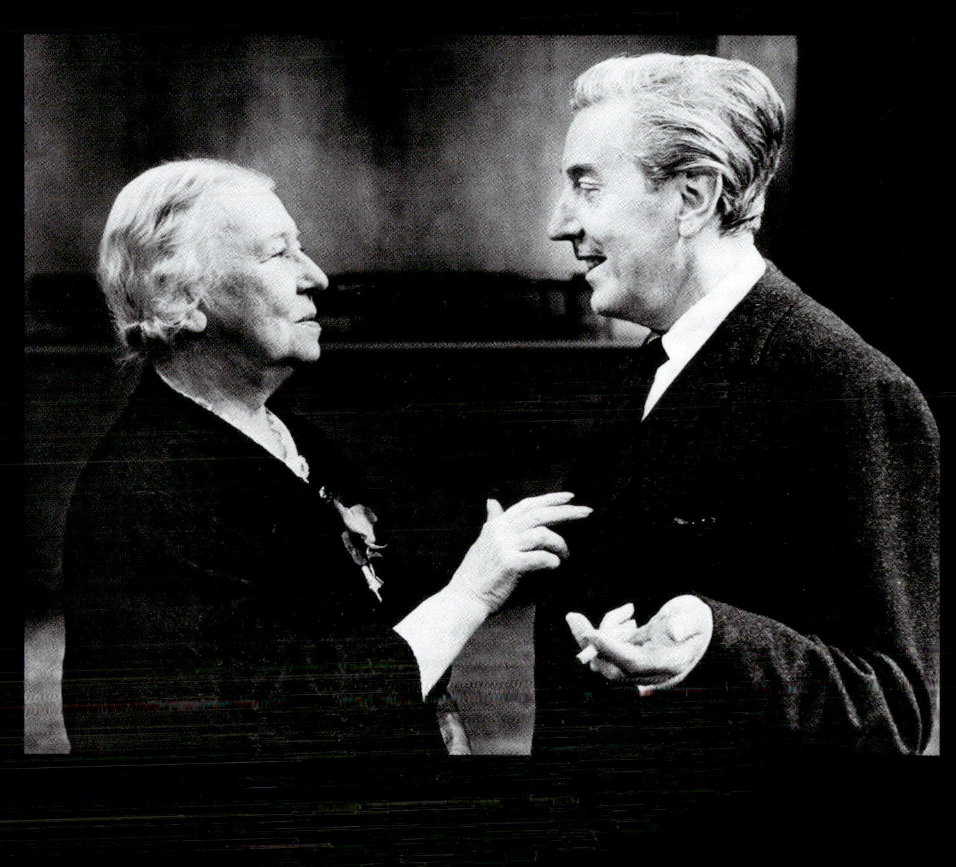

INTRODUCTION

I first came across Sergei Diaghilev and the Ballet Russes when I saw a revival of *L'après midi d'un faune* almost twenty-five years ago. What Nijinsky, Debussy, and Baskt achieved in a ballet that lasted no more than ten minutes was astonishing in its precision and intensity. After that, I read everything I could about the Ballet Russes, delving deeper into its rich and complex history. Diaghilev and his company managed to change the history of dance, music, and stage and costume design in a span of a few years. One of the company's most important works of the 1920s was *Les Noces.* I was familiar with Igor Stravinsky's score and had seen a couple of historical photos of the rehearsals; sketches and drawings by Natalia Goncharova were also widely reproduced. However, it was only when I saw a reconstruction of the ballet in a commercial video recording that I understood how everything came together to create a work of such shattering power. When it premiered in Paris in 1923, *Les Noces* caused a sensation. The original production, with choreography by Bronislava Nijinska, music by Stravinsky, and sets and costumes by Goncharova, remains one of the masterpieces of twentieth-century dance. Its influence on musicians, choreographers, artists, and scholars has had a far-reaching impact that continues to this day. In 1965 the renowned choreographer Frederick Ashton, then director of the Royal Ballet, saved *Les Noces* from oblivion by inviting Nijinska to come to London to stage it. Two young dancers from the Royal Ballet, Monica Mason and Christopher Newton, worked closely with Nijinska during the long and unique rehearsal period. They took part in the premiere of the revival in 1966. The following conversation took place in the offices of the Royal Ballet in London in January 2011.

—ARTURO HERRERA

Bronislava Nijinska and Frederick Ashton rehearsing *Les Noces* at the Royal Opera House, London. Photograph by Houston Rogers, 1966. © V&A Images

Arturo Herrera: *Les Noces* premiered in London in 1966. The rehearsals took several weeks. What was your role in this revival?

Christopher Newton: When I first auditioned for *Les Noces,* I was just a member of the corps de ballet. I was in Scene II, The Preparation of the Groom, which is the men's scene, and then Scene IV, The Wedding Feast, which is everybody together.

It was really quite strange for us to start working with Bronislava Nijinska. She didn't have much English at all. And the score ... we'd listen to the music, and we realized that it was going to be very complicated to do. But she was very precise about how *she* saw the music. She'd broken it down into "dancers' counts," which isn't necessarily what a musician would understand from the score. But dancers tend to count what they hear rather than what is written musically, and I think that's how she broke it down, as I say, into "dancers' counts," which fitted her choreography. She was getting to know the company, obviously—to know the dancers.

She was very, very specific about teaching each of the steps. She wouldn't go on from one step to the next until the first step that she taught was exactly as she wanted it. And because she was quite an elderly lady at the time, it was difficult for her, for one communicates dances visually, but because of her age, she was unable to do the steps absolutely full-out, as it were. So, she would give us an *idea* of it. We would do what she showed us, and then she would start pulling us and pushing us and putting us into the right positions and trying to explain exactly what she wanted. And therefore, it was really quite a slow process. She was mobile, but she was quite deaf. She had a rather ancient hearing aid that used to pick up static. She was very clear about what she wanted. And her musicality—the way she understood the music—was amazing.

AH: I read that she focused more on movement structure than in creating a linear narrative of a wedding in a peasant community in old Russia. This kind of exacting choreographic construction must have been hard to follow at the beginning. How long did this take, from the time she came and met with all of you until the premiere?

CN: I honestly don't remember, but it was quite slow. We were doing other work at the same time, so it was all mixed in with our current repertoire. It just gradually built. Monica might have a better idea—I'm terrible with dates! But you know, it's one of those things that you

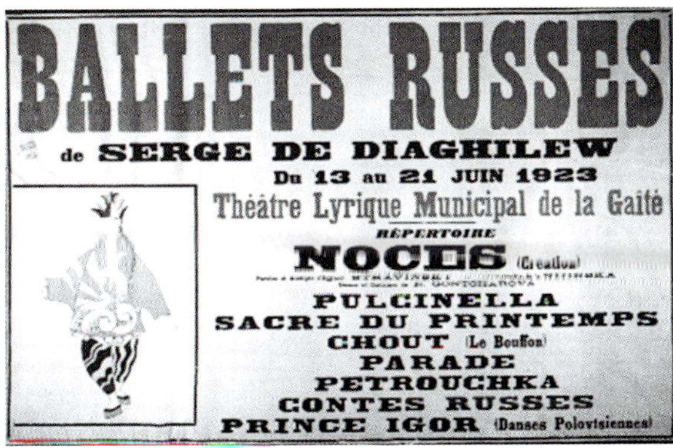

Poster advertising the premiere of *Les Noces* at the Théâtre de la Gaîte-Lyrique, Paris, June 13–21, 1923

didn't really bother about: you did your work and you went to rehearsals. You were called for a rehearsal, so you went and did it. And that was it.

AH: Your first role was in the corps de ballet, in The Preparation of the Groom, where the young man is anointed by his friends, and you were also in The Wedding Feast, where everyone dances euphorically until the tolling of a bell. Both of those scenes are full of twisting motions, arcs, runs, and jumps that seem primary and elemental but are incredible thrilling to watch. Later on, you also danced the part of the father, correct?

CN: Yes, after that, I then danced the part of the bride's father.

AH: Nijinska thought of *Les Noces* as a sacred drama, a severe, solemn piece driven by the rhythmic construction of the music. Except for a few rare moments of joy, she didn't want any emotions or individual characterizations.

CN: Absolutely.

AH: How was that for the young dancers?

CN: It was rather difficult because we were so used to putting our own interpretation on things. And she said, "No, no, no." She wanted an absolutely blank face, especially for the principals. I think that for Svetlana Beriosova, whom she adored, it was very difficult for her to keep her face absolutely immobile and not show any emotion. Even with an immobile face, you can still show emotion, but I think that's very, very hard.

AH: Was it painful to dance because the steps were so difficult? For instance, the parallel feet, the constructed pyramids, the rigid body, the emphasis on the collective?

CN: Not really. It was just so alien to anything else that we had ever done. From the men's point of view, Nijinska hated the men to point their feet, to stretch the foot. She just wanted it—

AH: Flat.

CN: Well, not flat. If I can demonstrate—she sort of just wanted it *left* there. You didn't point and you didn't flex. You just relaxed it somewhere in between, which we found very awkward to do, because you naturally want to either point your feet or flex your feet so that there's some sort of feeling of tension there. But if it's just relaxed, you think you're not doing anything.

AH: And was Nijinska's daughter Irina present during rehearsals?

CN: No. Her husband was there. He was not a dancer or anything. He was a strange little man, but he was always there in the studio, at her side. I don't know what function he had there, really.

AH: Nijinska attended all the rehearsals?

CN: Absolutely. She was totally in command.

AH: And she was also present for the premiere in London in 1966?

CN: Oh, yes. She actually told us that we did it better than the Russians!

AH: As for the austere minimalist sets: were they repainted according to Natalia Goncharova's original designs? And the abstract brown-and-white costumes that everybody wears, as well?

CN: Yes. From the original, but made new.

AH: And what was the reaction from the public? I read that it was a triumph.

CN: Yes, it was a success. It surprised us all, actually. Well, it amazed me because I thought the British public—the general ballet public that comes to the opera house—I don't think they had ever seen anything like it.

AH: Diaghilev brought it to London in 1926. It was heavily criticized.

CN: Badly received?

AH: Yes, it was attacked by the press. But after the first performance and the critics had had their say, H. G. Wells wrote an open letter addressing its significance, gravity, and sheer excitement, saying that it was such a powerful piece, which was then inserted into the programs at all subsequent productions.

I'd like to hear more about the heritage of the Ballet Russes. Was Diaghilev and the whole legacy of Nijinsky and Stravinsky's music—was that something that intrigued the young dancers when this idea came up at the school?

CN: We had already done quite a lot of the Diaghilev repertoire. Serge Grigoriev, who was Diaghilev's ballet master, put on *The Firebird* for us—in 1954, I think. I was still a student at the school when we first did that. It was actually probably 1953. And then he did *Les Sylphides, Petrushka,* and he did the Polovtsian Dances from *Prince Igor.* They were all put on by Serge Grigoriev and his wife, Lubov Tchernicheva. When I was a student, we were also doing some of Massine's pieces. We were doing *Le Tricorne.* And later we did *The Good-Humored Ladies*—"*Les Femmes de Bonne Humeur.*"

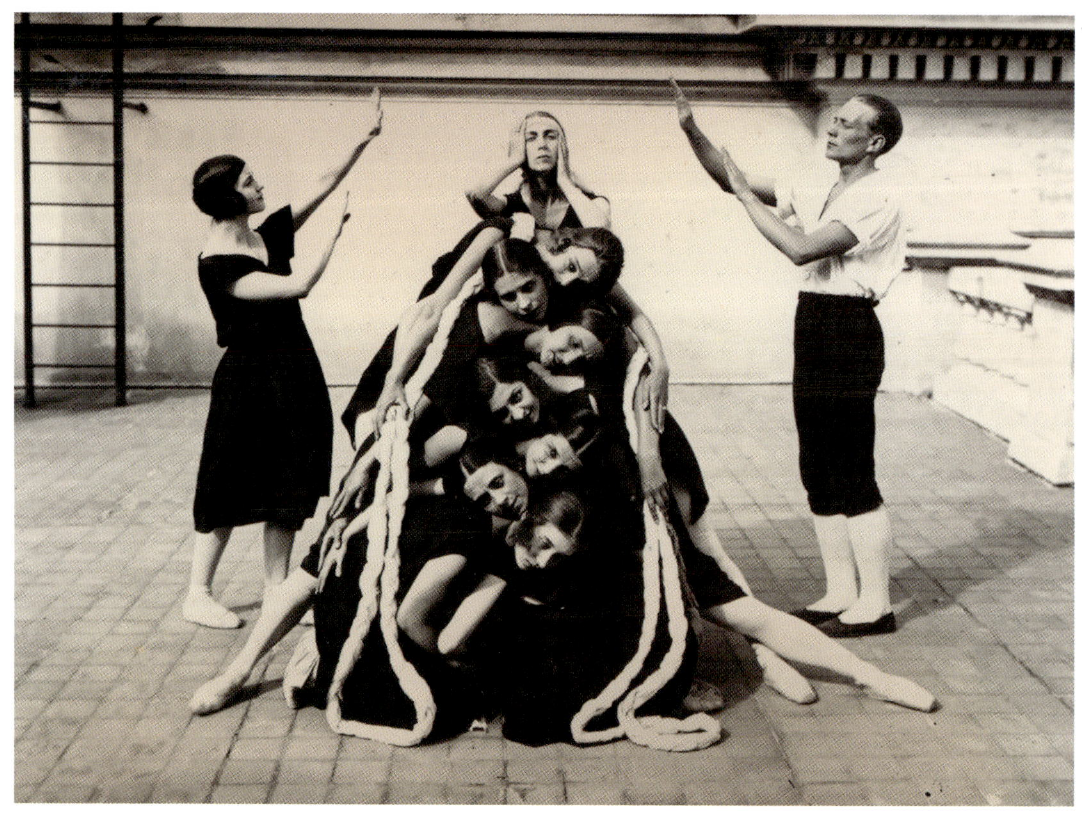

Rehearsal of *Les Noces* on the roof of the Théâtre de Monte-Carlo, 1923. Bronislava Nijinska Collection, Music Division, Library of Congress

AH: What about *Les Biches?*

CN: That's a Nijinska piece. We did *Les Biches* around the same time. I'm not sure whether it was before *Les Noces* or after *Les Noces.* But we did *Les Biches* and *Les Noces* virtually one year after the other. You know, one season we did one piece, and the following season we did the other.

AH: When *Les Noces* came into the repertoire, it was like another part of this legendary Ballet Russes tradition.

CN: It was always exciting to do a new piece. It was very interesting, you know, especially *Les Noces,* which was so totally different from anything else we'd ever done.

AH: Some of Nijinska's steps, especially the crouching-in, jumps, and ritual groupings, bring to mind those of her brother, Vaslav Nijinsky, and *The Rite of Spring.* How exhausting was *Les Noces* for each of you?

CN: It's not exhausting, as such. It's just—especially when you get to the final scene—

AH: The Wedding Feast.

CN: Yes, Scene IV. It's what I would call relentless. It goes on, on, on, on. It doesn't stop! But it's not physically exhausting, per se.

AH: It looks very demanding. The entire corps of people dancing up and down, bodies flying, fists clenching, geometric formations, and this ever-present downward pull.

CN: Dancers nowadays are much more used to being physically tired. They have much longer roles. I don't ever remember being physically tired in it at all, but the weight of the piece, it is very—

AH: Mechanical.

CN: —it's very mechanical, yes, but it's also very "into the ground," you know. Dancers want to be light, but one of the things that Nijinska was always saying was, "Down, down, down!"

AH: Can you tell me more about your role as *répétiteur* for this piece?

CN: I was making the transition from dancer to working in the studio with the dancers and coaching and being *répétiteur.* Because I've got a very retentive memory, I was called upon to take rehearsals and reteach the new dancers. A *répétiteur* is just a French name for a ballet master.

AH: So, you had a very clear memory of the steps?

CN: Yes, I was able to teach it, and I wrote it down, as well.

AH: Is that part of the role of the *répétiteur,* too?

CN: Not necessarily. But it's very helpful if a ballet master knows the notation system, because then he can read a score and pass it on to the dancers. But the one thing I've always been very, very conscious of is the fact that, although one notates it, one also must try to carry out the intentions of the choreographer. And it's not necessarily evident in the notation. Having worked with Nijinska, one knows what her intentions were within a piece. Not just what the steps were physically, but what her *intention* was. And that's what I always tried to pass on.

She was very adamant about certain steps and movements. I remember when we were doing Scene II, The Preparation of the Groom, and Michael Somes was the ballet master at the time. There were two rows of men, three and three. And they were directly behind each other, in two rows, but one of the boys in the second row wasn't directly behind the boy in front of him. He was pushed over into the space. And Michael Somes said to her, "That boy isn't in line with the ones in front, like the other two are." And she said, "No, no, no, this is not *Swan Lake*!" She wanted it specifically to be like that—for one boy to be out of line with the rest of the group.

AH: Asymmetrically?

CN: Well, it's not really asymmetrical—it's totally out of line! Those are the sorts of things that I'm very keen on, because these kinds of details can, in time, get ironed out. Each time it gets repeated, somebody thinks, "Oh, that doesn't look right, we'll put it right." But that was, in fact, the way she wanted it.

AH: If I had a company and wanted to recreate *Les Noces*, how would I go about it?

CN: We have our complete notation score here. What we try to do within the Royal Ballet is to pass it on down to the next generation and then the next generation, and to make sure that they are very accurate with it so that they transmit a very important heritage to any company. That way we maintain the integrity of the piece. *Les Noces* has been done by other companies around the world, and for me, anyway, they're not as accurate as the production that Nijinska herself actually gave to us.

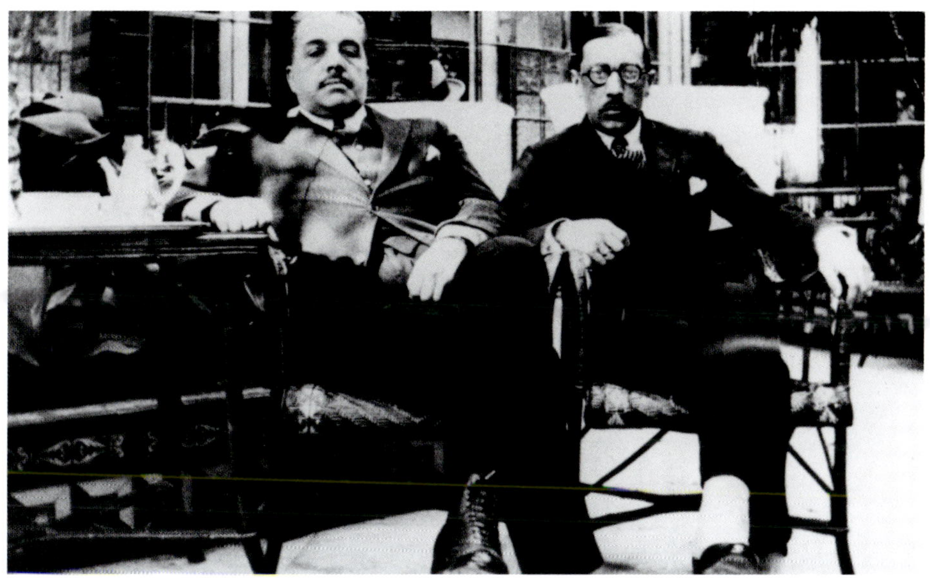

Serge Diaghilev (left) and Igor Stravinsky (right), Paris, France, 1921. V & A Theatre Collection

AH: Many choreographers have used the music and done different choreographies.

CN: Oh, yes. And they have also done Nijinska's production themselves. ... I know there's somebody who's done it for San Francisco Ballet who took it from what was taught to the Paris Opera Ballet. And it sort of—it gets changed as it goes on. Do you see what I mean? It was taught to the Paris Opera company by somebody who had been in it here. But Nijinska herself wasn't there. So, although it was fairly well done, there were certain things in it that went against what she had taught the Royal Ballet.

AH: In 1965 Frederick Ashton asked Nijinska to come to London to stage *Les Noces,* and in 1966 the revival finally happened. Do you have any idea how this came about? Was it Frederick Ashton's personal interest in the piece?

Monica Mason: Fred was directing. He started to direct in 1963.

CN: Yes. And he must have seen *Les Noces* and *Les Biches* when Diaghilev had done it.

MM: Yes. I remember there was a little company meeting, and he explained that we were going to have with us this wonderful woman. And she was, in his opinion, one of the greatest choreographers in the world. He said it was a great honor to have her with us, and that we were all to work as hard as we could for her. He warned us that she didn't speak English. He said, "It won't be easy. The music is tricky. But, in my opinion, it's one of the greatest ballets ever created. And I want you all to really pay attention, to work very hard for her." And that, I remember, was a very clear instruction as to how we were going to behave. Of course, because one had such respect for Frederick Ashton, if he said that somebody was, "in his opinion," one of the greatest choreographers of all time, you sort of thought, well, "Wow. This person must be very special." So, there was never any doubting it, was there?

Not that we did. I mean, I was still young in 1963, but very often, if a new person came in, you formed your own opinion. But in this instance, we just bought into it lock, stock, and barrel. That was how I felt about it.

So, when she arrived, I just thought, thank goodness he warned us. Because she was really without English. She had little French words, and she had Russian and Polish, I imagine. But it was really up to everybody in the room to be as focused as they could at all times.

Of course, for us it was tough, because like any choreographer, she was only interested in *her* ballet. She didn't care that we had *Swan Lake* that night, or we'd had *Swan Lake* the night before, or that we might be a little tired or anything. She just demanded one hundred percent concentration and work and focus. And she was very loath to give little breaks, because in those days, the unions weren't as organized as they are now, so you didn't have a cutoff point in a rehearsal where you had to stop for a break. But, if we were going for three hours with her, there came a point where you were absolutely gasping. And of course, in those days, there were no bottles of water allowed in the studio, no drinking. So, we used to get thirsty! And it was only the boys, whom she loved more than the girls, naturally—

CN: Oh, yes!

MM: —whom she would allow to suggest a tea break. And that became, for the boys, sort of a little joke. What was hard was having a rehearsal with her when it was only girls—then, she used to go straight through regardless of any breaks. And we used to be gasping at the end! But what was really astonishing was the way that the piece came together from a woman who was no longer young.

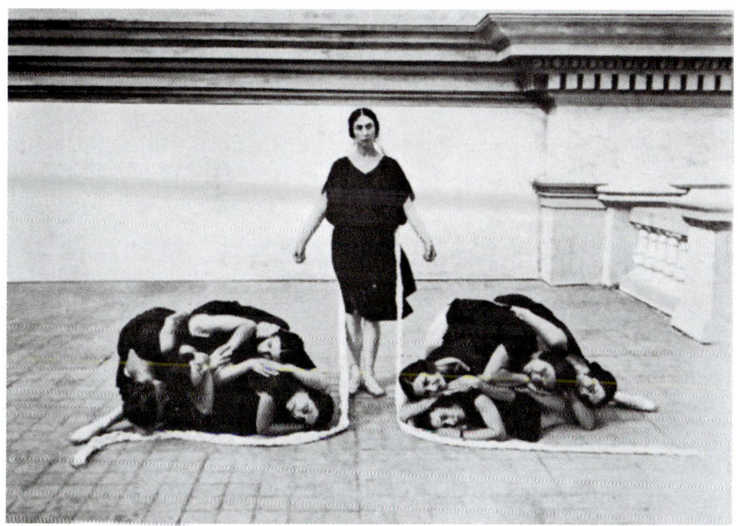

Rehearsal of *Les Noces* on the roof of the Théâtre de Monte-Carlo, 1923. Bronislava Nijinska Collection, Music Division, Library of Congress

CN: She wasn't physically able to show us anything—

MM: No, she didn't.

CN: —but she pushed us and pulled us.

AH: Sono Osato, a dancer with the Ballet Russes, wrote that at night, in her dreams, she would hear the counts and Nijinska's voice shouting repeatedly, "*Zemla! Zemla!* Earth! Earth!"

MM: She communicated that somehow, and I think one of the things that one got so much from her was the *weight* of the piece, the sort of—

CN: Into the ground—

MM: Yes, the "into-the-groundness." That was a total departure from anything else we'd ever done. I mean, it was not like anything else we'd known. Oh, we'd done Fokine. I mean, Fokine ballets were neoclassical. But Nijinska ... of course, one wonders whether her brother was an influence on her, and whether they were trying, really, to explore what they would eventually call modern dance—you know, parallel feet and a sense of weight into the floor, which was absolutely contrary to the whole classical style.

CN: We dancers are normally trying to lift ourselves *off* the floor.

MM: Yes, we try to lift off the floor and create this lightness. But everything was weighted—and of course it was because of the subject, really, because what she was exploring was peasant dancing in a classical format.

AH: Exactly. An archaic but abstract ceremony of rebirth.

MM: So, I think that we understood the sort of—the *solemnity* of this peasant wedding, which was not about anything frivolous or light. It was focused on the superstitions and the *ritual* aspect of the wedding.

CN: Let's not forget the fact that she wanted absolutely no emotion, like we said earlier on.

MM: Yes, no facial expression. *No* facial expression. That was very interesting.

CN: And the way we held our bodies, as well. It wasn't upright. We were—you know, we were, sort of—

MM: *Rounded.*

CN: And the hands were very specifically not stretched, not clenched, but sort of somewhere in the middle. And I was explaining about the boys' feet, that she never wanted the boys to either point their feet or flex them.

MM: They were just relaxed.

CN: They sort of flopped around on the end of your leg. It was really quite a strange feeling to have to do that.

AH: She is one of the great choreographers of all time. Was that something that you knew then, or did you only realize it later on?

MM: I think dancers, generally, are ... we certainly were in the raw about it. First of all, we were used to a lot of new work from Ashton, and even from MacMillan, as early as the mid-1960s. We were used to making lots of new pieces. So, we were used to being very disciplined about serving the choreographer—about just being an empty vessel, really. And you *served*—that was your duty: you didn't have an opinion; you weren't asked to express interest or not; you simply were there to do as you were told—to do what they asked you to do. So, I think it was fascinating to know that she was, obviously, as I've said, one of Fred's huge influences.

We had to concentrate very hard, because it was extremely difficult to do what she wanted us to do. And if you didn't do what she wanted you to do, she got very angry—so much more angry and irritable and impatient than I ever saw Frederick Ashton or even Kenneth MacMillan.

CN: Because they worked by sort of drawing something *out* of you, didn't they? But she was absolutely pedantic as to what she wanted to put *into* you.

MM: Yes. Yes, that's right. And she demanded that you just *serve* her. You served the cause.

AH: Which was a completely different way of working?

MM: It was new for all of us. And I think it was probably only when we did the ballet. I remember having fittings for the costumes and thinking, this is not a ballet where there is one *jot* of glamour! We are *not* going to look beautiful! I do remember, however, that she was very insistent on the way we tied the headscarves. And all of us used to sit together and try to get them in just the right place. We managed to tie them as elegantly as possible, and even shape them a little—to put a hairpin in and poke the shape of it so that it was a bit more enhancing. But we never knew whether she was going to come up and catch us, and of course, because she didn't have English, she would be rattling off in something else. And the costumes were brown and white. Everybody wore the same colors. But of course, after the first night, the reviews were wonderful.

CN: Incredible.

MM: Absolutely rave reviews.

CN: It remains one of the greatest ballets, certainly.

MM: We were reassured. And if we had *any* doubts, which I don't think we had, by the time we got to the first night—

CN: I don't remember having doubts—not at all. I just remember trying to do—

MM: —trying to do everything—

CN: —the absolute best one could possibly do.

MM: The most terrifying thing was the finale, when you're in lines across the stage, where every mistake looks so big.

CN: If you're sitting out front, and you can see one person out of fifty people onstage, you can see that person making a mistake.

MM: Because everybody was dressed so simply.

CN: And that's what terrifies you when you're doing it, because you know how vulnerable you are.

AH: I also know that some of the men and women danced the same steps. It is like a genderless ballet.

MM: Yes, we did a lot of the same steps. The positions of the arms were the same for men and women. Girls were *en pointe,* so we did point our feet—not like relaxed feet for the boys. But again, the skirts were long and the feet were brown, so you didn't feel very pretty! Nothing felt pretty. But it was fascinating and intriguing.

AH: Diaghilev was very pleased with Nijinska's initial suggestion that *Les Noces* be danced *en pointe.* She wanted the women tapping into this connection to the earth; she didn't want to elongate the leg or the feet but to go down all the time—to make it very physical, almost sexual.

MM: Little stabbing movements.

AH: Yes, like a hard tapping on the stage floor.

MM: Yes.

AH: How were the roles assigned?

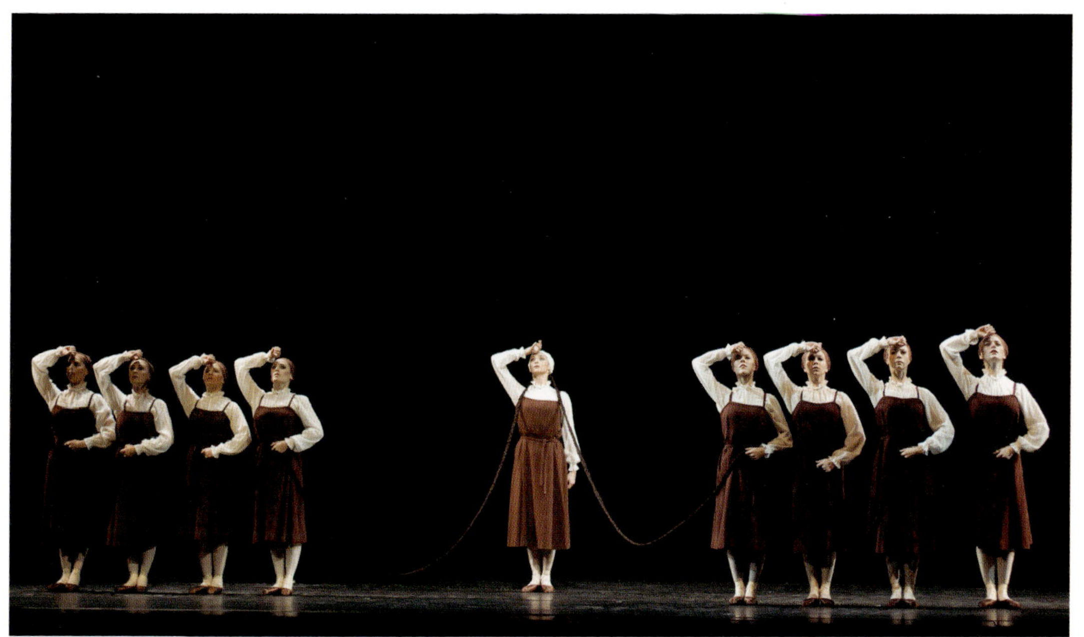

Scene I: Consecration of the Bride, from the ballet *Les Noces,* performed at the Royal Ballet, London, 2004. Photograph by Bill Cooper

CN: I think she started off, if I remember correctly, by having the whole company in the studio. And she chose certain people to do things based on their looks more than anything, I think, didn't she? Because I remember people like Alexander Grant being there, and David Blair, who were principals, and they eventually got eliminated, didn't they?

MM: Yes.

CN: It was really quite strange.

AH: But don't dancers have to be selected according to a specific height?

CN: She did some things that were really quite strange. I don't know whether she had—she must have had—I'm certain she had favorites, didn't she? But when we'd been in groups and lines, say, and then changed the total pattern, she would make people go from one side of the stage to the other. It wasn't a logical progression from one pattern to the next. She would push people around until she got them where she wanted them. And it's one of the things now that I still do when I teach it. I could quite easily make it logical—

MM: And symmetrical.

CN: —but I don't. I keep it the way that Nijinska actually did it. So, these people that got pushed from pillar to post then still get pushed from pillar to post now! She *put* people where she wanted them.

MM: Yes. Irrespective—

CN: —irrespective of the pattern. There is that point in the beginning of The Wedding Feast where it goes into what we used to call "garage doors," where the whole thing sort of closes in on itself. And people had to juggle themselves to get into the right place; it doesn't happen logically.

AH: This ballet has a bride and a groom, but they really don't act as protagonists. Individualism was not encouraged. It's really the *group* that moves the whole ballet into this frantic, *fortissimo,* perfectly impersonal kind of piece. How long would the rehearsals last?

MM: Probably for three hours at a time.

AH: How long did they continue until the premiere?

MM: Oh, I would have thought we must have had a couple of months—I can't remember. Two months at least.

CN: I don't know whether it happens to other dancers, but as for the preparation of any piece ... for me, once you've got the piece completed and you get to the opening night, everything else that's gone before it gets wiped out. What you focus on, then, is the finished product. That's it. Often, *how* we get there, for me, gets lost. It's not something I retain. What I retain is the final product.

MM: That's right. Well, because also, especially in a piece like this, because it had been created before—forty years before or whatever it was—somehow, she must have kept notes to remind herself. I don't know how *exactly* the same it was as it had been when she created it. Who's to say? Nobody would know.

I remember that I made her very angry one day. I never meant to; it was just that she thought I was trying to get out of a repeated kneel. It was in the beginning of the first movement. We repeated and repeated and repeated this kneeling step, and the next day, I came into work and my knees had swelled. I couldn't straighten my leg and I couldn't kneel. So, I thought, well, I'll just have to take it easy for a day and it will settle down, which of course it did. That day, I said to the man who was assisting her, Michael Somes, "Michael, I'm very sorry, you can see what's happened to my knees." And he said. "Good lord, what have you done?" And I said, "I think it was all the kneeling yesterday. Please, could you tell Madame that I'll dance but that I can't kneel?"

And she looked at me like—[glares]—and then she said something to Michael and I heard him say, "Monica Mason." And with that she walked over to her husband and he took his little book out and opened it up and wrote, I assume, "Monica Mason" and shut the book and put it away. And so I was allowed not to do it, but I think she thought I was shirking. I think she thought I was trying to get out of it.

Well, of course by the next day I was fine again, so I went back in. But she always looked at me like that. She terrified me, because I was not a naughty girl—I was a good girl! And I didn't like being thought of as naughty or trying not to work or something because it wasn't true. But she ... ooh. And you could tell: once she got an idea in her head, that was it!

AH: It was final.

MM: Forever. I remember that moment and I can see her now looking at me and I can feel the guilt and I saw the book come out and the name ... I can see all of that like yesterday. But I also think that—like Christopher says—you don't really remember a great deal about the rehearsal period, because we were all concentrating so hard on getting it right for her. And it was a huge mountain to climb. It was not an easy task.

CN: No, it wasn't. I just remember one incident from it, and that was when we were starting with Scene IV and we started with the very, very first steps—

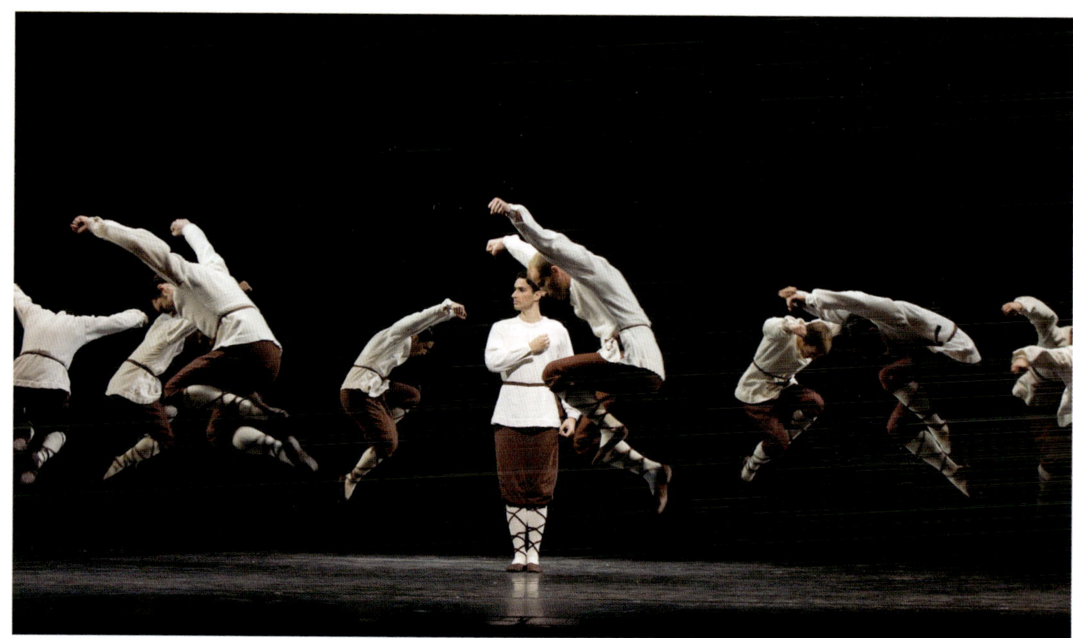

Scene II: Consecration of the Groom, from the ballet *Les Noces,* performed at the Royal Ballet, London, 2004. Photograph by Bill Cooper

AH: The Wedding Feast?

CN: Yes. For the men, the opening sequence. She taught it to us and we did it. And then she started going on with something else, and I just sort of relaxed—you know, how you relax a bit when she'd moved on to something else. I was probably chatting to somebody, quietly, in the corner. And she suddenly latched on to the fact that we weren't concentrating on *her.* So she looked at me and said, "Do it." I said, "What?" And she said she wanted me to do what she thought I hadn't bothered to learn. Since I learn things pretty quickly, I just did it, and she was, in fact, really quite impressed. So, from then on, it was like—I was not one of the chosen few but I was *something.*

AH: In the ballet, one of the most striking things is the dancing *en pointe* at the beginning of Scene I, The Bride's Chamber—these relentlessly vertical, downward stabs and the arms firmly keeping the body in place like Byzantine saints.

MM: It's really reflecting the music.

AH: For the audience, it looks rather painful!

MM: There's a relentless sort of a rhythm to it. But no, the pointe work—I wouldn't say the pointe work was especially difficult. It was just part of the whole thing. It was the style. It was this weighted, turned-in, different way of using your arms, different way of using your body. And, of course, no expression.

All of that was very difficult, because when you come to Scene IV, it is a celebration. The movements said everything. And of course, that was what became part of the ritual of it. There were no individuals; it was a body of people. I see it now and I just think I'm so grateful that I was part of it and I learned it and that I met her. I have these memories because, I think when you're young, too, your memories are very vivid. But those early memories. ... At that age, you're in your twenties, and what do you know? You know very little. So, when somebody great like that comes along, they make the most indelible impression on you.

AH: The men's jumps in the center—during Scene II, The Preparation of the Groom, were they especially difficult to do in a circle?

CN: Yes, it is very difficult to get the actual sequence of it, because it has a repetition to it, but it's sort of irregular and you have to know where the irregularities are to get it right. And invariably, somebody got this wrong.

AH: How did the dancers keep time with this unusual music, made up of six percussionists, four pianists, four vocal soloists, and a choir?

CN: Keeping time is not the problem, no. It's learning the sequence.

MM: It's learning the music.

CN: Dancers relate it to the music: if the *music* isn't right, then *they* aren't right. Say we're in a rehearsal situation with just a pianist, and the pianist hits the wrong note, the dancers immediately know that the pianist has gone wrong because they are so used to hearing what they dance to. Even if just a couple of notes go wrong, they hear it.

MM: It throws the dance.

AH: Nijinska wanted her choreography to be architectural. She thought of her piece as a complete entity having its own voice, without imitating Stravinsky's asymmetrical rhythms and measures. How did you handle that—learning steps that seem autonomous to that powerful, coherent score? Because, like you said, there was no room for interpretation.

MM: I think you do it just by being a very disciplined creature. You do as you're told. It's rather similar to learning a Shakespeare speech, something very lengthy. The word is there on the page, and you can't insert other words. You have to say the words that are there. The same applies to music. Musicians are absolutely skilled and disciplined and trained to read those notes on that score, not to play what they feel like playing or even how they feel like playing it. They play it the way the conductor has rehearsed it, and then they focus and concentrate to bring it alive. I think that was what was remarkable: knowing that this piece had been made all these years before and that it had been done somewhere else. But we were the first people to do it after the 1920s, you know, so it was the knowledge that this wonderful work was being brought back to life. We felt a tremendous responsibility.

CN: Well, Fred instilled it in us.

MM: Fred really knew this was a great work, so it was up to us to make it so. We just knew that was the order.

AH: *Les Noces* reveals a Constructivist influence in its use of movement as a dynamic force, gymnastics, and architectural forms. Was that hard for the young dancers—these groupings of diagonal or parallel formations?

CN: Sometimes, it was difficult to get into the positions that she wanted. But the actual shapes and things were—

MM: I think that was so beautifully constructed.

CN: Yes, absolutely.

MM: I think she made it so brilliant that there emerged a logic, and there was a physicality that was possible to capture.

CN: Sometimes, she asked you to do something that you felt was a little bit physically *impossible,* didn't she? I mean especially the girls in those opening groups. Those terrible sideways positions. You could get into the position but then had to stay there. I did find those sorts of things a bit difficult. And the end—the circle you were talking about at the end of the men's scene—she wanted your back to be absolutely flat, parallel to the ground, but to jump in that position as well—to jump without straightening your body is very difficult.

AH: I've seen on DVD the BBC's filming of the Royal Ballet's *Les Noces,* staged at Covent Garden in 2001, and all the dancers are devoid of expression, as requested by Nijinska. That, combined with the complex architecture of the choreography, gives the audience the feeling that a Herculean effort was being undertaken onstage.

CN: I didn't find it exhausting but, as I said earlier, the relentlessness of it was difficult. It sort of went on and on and on. You didn't get tired, but it was just the actual difficulty of having to do it.

MM: We got very hot, but not exhausted. And challenged mentally.

AH: Can you tell me more about that?

MM: Well, it's because Stravinsky is not regular.

CN: There are some really irregular jumps that we used to get in the boys' scene. You count seven-one, and then you'd only have half a beat at the end of the phrase instead of a full beat. But that's the way it fitted into the choreography—not necessarily the way that musicians played it.

AH: And who gives that cue?

MM: Nijinska gave that. She knew every single breath of that music. And she couldn't bear for you not to be absolutely *with* the music, because that's what clearly drove her: the rhythm. These extraordinary rhythms of the music.

CN: And there are moments when the dancing goes totally *across* the rhythm of the music as well, which one found very difficult to do, because you felt like you were *fighting* the music rather than going with it. It didn't happen very often, but it does happen in the boys' scenes.

MM: Yes. I can't think of a moment, an instance, necessarily. ...

CN: It just happens a couple of times in the men's Scene II. Right at the very beginning. When we're in that circle and there's all that stamping. Some of that goes against the music.

MM: Yes. This expressionless thing, I was intrigued by it because I was always, especially as a young dancer, very animated and probably a bit over-the-top. But to have to control it like that was really something.

She rarely used that in *Les Biches* because she didn't allow you to rely on your face to communicate—it was the choreography, the music, the style that she'd created. *Les Biches* was far harder to dance than *Les Noces* in terms of technical challenge, but you created it in your body. You didn't rely on pulling faces or looking at the audience or anything. She couldn't bear any of that.

There is a wonderful moment in *Les Biches* when the hostess, having danced herself into quite a frenzy, collapses on the sofa, and these two beautiful young men come into the room, and she wants to beckon them toward her. Of course, in both *Les Noces* and *Les Biches* Nijinska worked with Svetlana Beriosova, who was one of the dancers we hugely admired. Svetlana was born in Lithuania. She spoke Russian, and so she spoke to Nijinska and then would turn to us and say, "Madame says," or "Madame wants you to understand," or "Madame would like to ask you to please think about, or to do this." One day, she was describing how she wanted the hostess to call these two young men closer to the sofa, but she wanted it all done by moving the head. So, we said to Svetlana, "Please ask Madame if she would show us. Would she do it for us?" We went to the front of the room and she sat on this little wooden chair—I can see it now—and complete magic happened. It was so brilliant, and I remember thinking at the time, if only we could film this and play it. Because of course, once it was finished, it was gone. We asked, would she do it again? And she said no—that was it; she'd done it once for us. And I don't think she ever did it again. But I can see—at least I *think* I can see—what she did in merely a few seconds, which was so profound in terms of what it was possible to express by doing nearly nothing. It was amazing, and I think this then brings us back to *Les Noces,* because, although we are doing lots—it's not that we were doing nothing—it was very often the simplest ... in a sense, not the *dance* movements but the *breathing* moments—

CN: —that expressed the whole *feel* of the thing.

MM: And you thought, how extraordinary—what is that? But you did it. You just did it because that's what you were instructed to do. You didn't even stop to think, do I believe in this or do I like it or do I think it's going to work? You just did it. And then, by and by, you could see that, with the whole room breathing, what an amazing sort of *wave* of movement there was.

AH: I'm not a dancer, but my feeling is that this ballet has a certain kind of sadness to it. It's like *The Rite of Spring,* which is another type of sacrificial ritual. Here, the bride and groom are joined in marriage for the benefit of the community. They don't know each other and yet they're going into this room together. Were you conceptually *in* the piece when you were dancing, knowing it was so terrifying?

MM: No, that's too psychological. I think that's what you appreciate later in life. And I think perhaps for me, coming from where you're coming, you would be examining it from that point of view. But dancers can't take all of that into their brains, and in fact, even if you were to try to express that, I don't know that it would contribute anything much, because it's the *choreographer* that's done that work. She devises the steps that express *her* innermost thoughts. She just requires somebody to do what she instructs. And of course what is interesting for choreographers—this happened with Ashton and MacMillan and Balanchine and everybody—they ask you to do something and then they say, "No, that actually doesn't work," because they can see that their idea is not coming across the way that they intended it to.

AH: Going back to this conceptual idea of dance: Balanchine absolutely refused to do anything with this music or with *The Rite of Spring.* He thought neither should ever be done, because both pieces were "unchoreographable." But he was a Russian choreographer, and the people that have done it since then have not been Russian. Merce Cunningham tried it, as well as Jerome Robbins.

MM: Jerome Robbins's production was beautiful.

AH: Yes, I saw it. Actually, if I remember correctly, he had second thoughts about his production after seeing the original.

MM: I'm sure.

AH: It was also taken up by a French choreographer?

MM: Yes, Angelin Preljocaj.

AH: What do you think it is about this score—what is its power—that keeps attracting young choreographers?

MM: It's a great piece of music.

CN: Even when you just listen to it without watching the ballet, it's an incredible piece of music in itself.

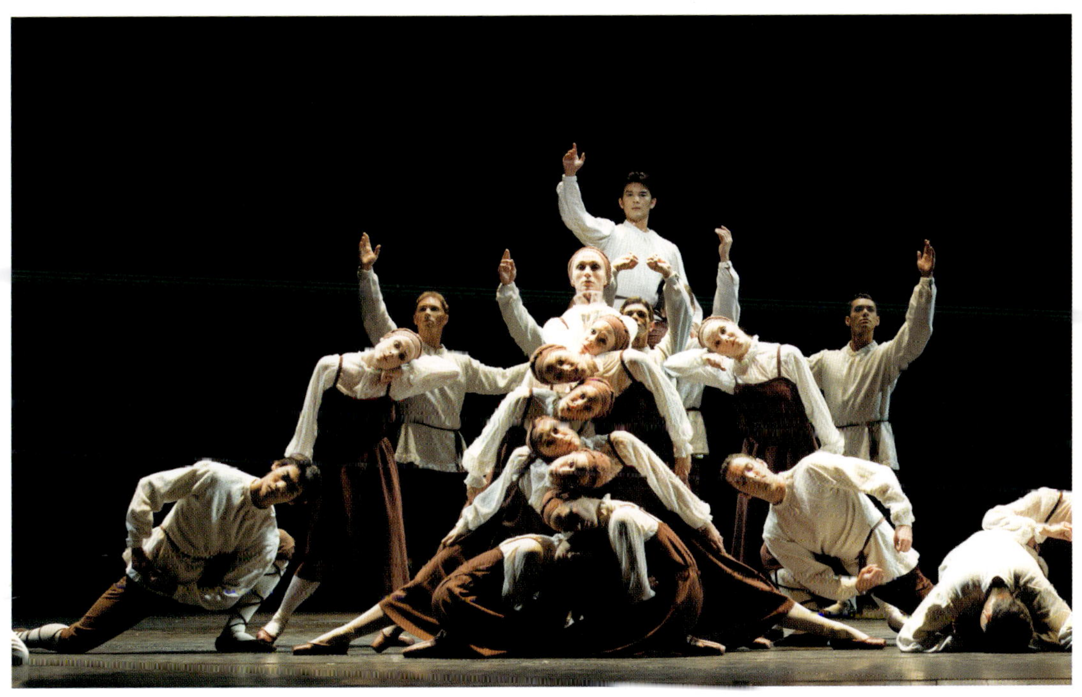

Scene IV: The Wedding Feast, from the ballet *Les Noces*, performed at the Royal Ballet, London, 2004. Photograph by Bill Cooper

MM: It's great art. And I think that, when choreographers hear a piece of music like that, for someone who loves to create and wants to create, one wants the challenge of matching a great score. And you know that you're inspired by the score. You want to try to make something wonderful. But I think Jerome Robbins probably meant it in all honesty that he felt this was a great score. He wanted the challenge and he did it and then he saw the original and thought, oy vey.

CN: In 1967 we were both doing *Les Noces* at the same time in New York.

MM: Yes, we were doing it at the Met, and the New York City Ballet was doing it across the square, at the State Theater.

CN: Yes. I know that the pianists were doing it first at the State Theater and then coming over to the Met.

MM: Yes, we were sharing the pianists.

CN: And they used to like his production better because they were actually on stage, whereas our pianists were in the pit!

AH: The Royal Ballet's production of *Les Noces* is available on the Internet; you can also buy the DVD. The company's interpretation had Nijinska's approval, since she taught the piece to you here in London, and now you celebrate its continuity.

CN: Well, that's what it's all about, really, isn't it—passing it on to the next generation.

MM: And communicating it to new dancers.

CN: Communicating exactly what it's all about.

MM: And they will find it as difficult as we found it. They might even find it *more* difficult in some ways.

AH: Why is that? Aren't dancers more athletic now? Don't they train in a greater variety of techniques and musical styles?

CN: I think they pick things up quicker now than we ever used to, don't they?

MM: Yes, they learn quicker.

CN: Therefore, they've got to find what the piece is about. We'll find out when we do *Les Noces* again.

MM: We will find out how they view it and how they settle into doing it. I think they'll probably love it because the music is so wonderful. We'll show them and talk to them about it. And they'll be inspired by the piece, because we will also say to them what Frederick Ashton said to us, and they will know that they are very fortunate to have the opportunity to be part of this. And they will know that I've chosen this ballet right at the very end of my directorship and how special it is to us, and how it's regarded in the world of dance. The company here is very respectful, and they will know that they're taking part in something very special.

I think the thing about *Les Noces* is—or what is wonderful right to the very end—is that you have danced very fully and you are hot and your brain has worked like mad, but then right at the very end it's like standing in church. It's like you feel like you're ... praising. You're giving thanks or you're praising the Lord or life or whatever it is that you believe in. You're thanking and you're honoring and, yes, it's a most wonderful feeling.

AH: Music critics talk about the pauses in between the tolling of the bell as one of the most compelling combinations of silence and sound in the history of dance, because the audience doesn't know how it's going to end. The music dies in a strangely lifting radiant close, as if we have been through this kind of—celebration, or ritual, and this pyramid is being formed on the dark stage. We feel part of a continuous cycle that is larger than us.

MM: How did you come to be so interested in *Les Noces*?

AH: I don't know. I just... .

MM: It just did something to you?

AH: It trapped me.

DAME MONICA MASON joined the Royal Ballet in 1958 and was appointed Director in 2002.

CHRISTOPHER NEWTON joined the Royal Ballet in 1954. He now works internationally as a freelance teacher.

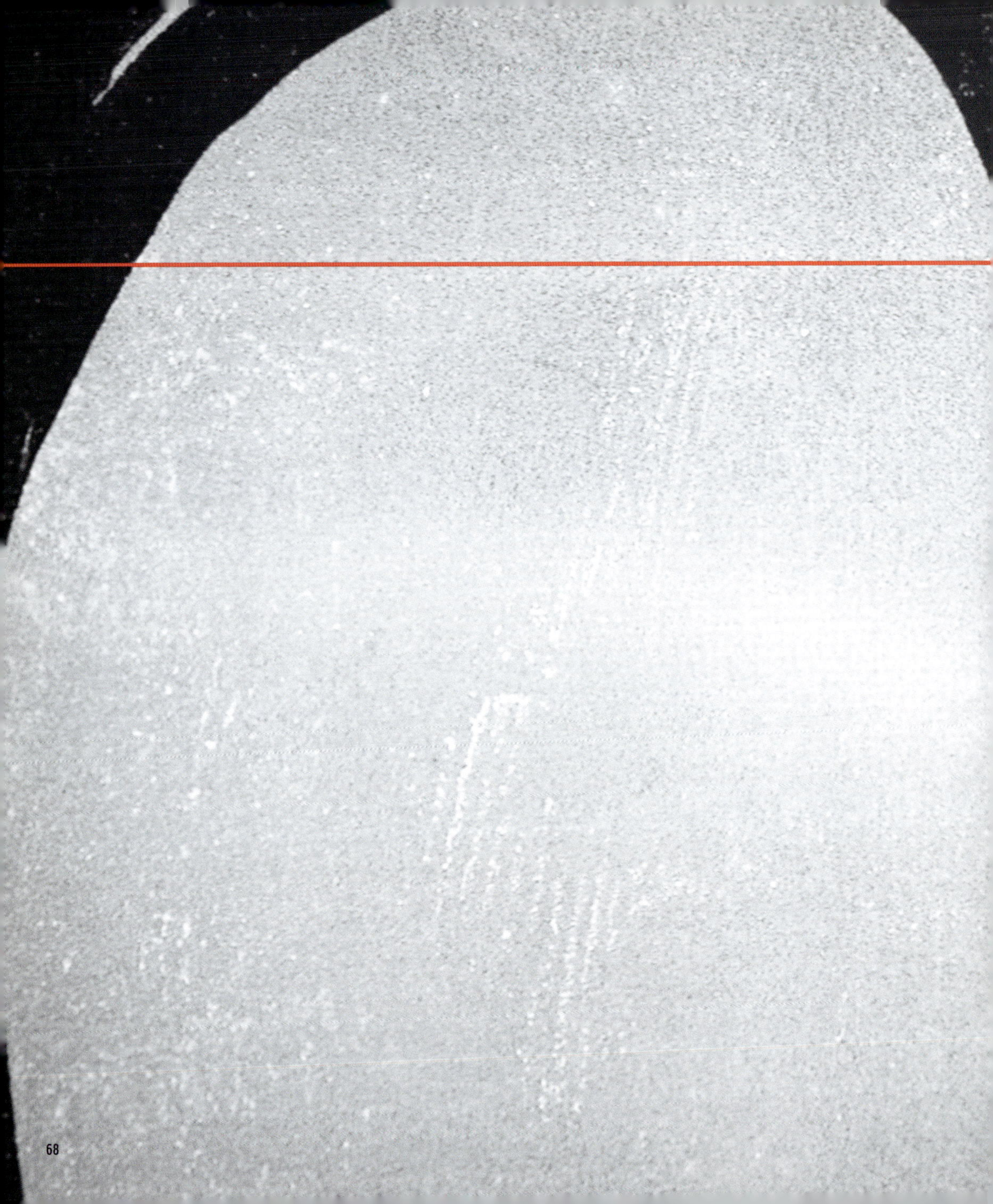

PLATES

1. *Les Noces* (The Wedding), 2007
Digital projection
Music: *Les Noces* by Igor Stravinsky, 1923
Performed by the Pokrovsky Ensemble
Elektra Nonesuch/Explorer Series, 1994
Collection of the artist, Berlin

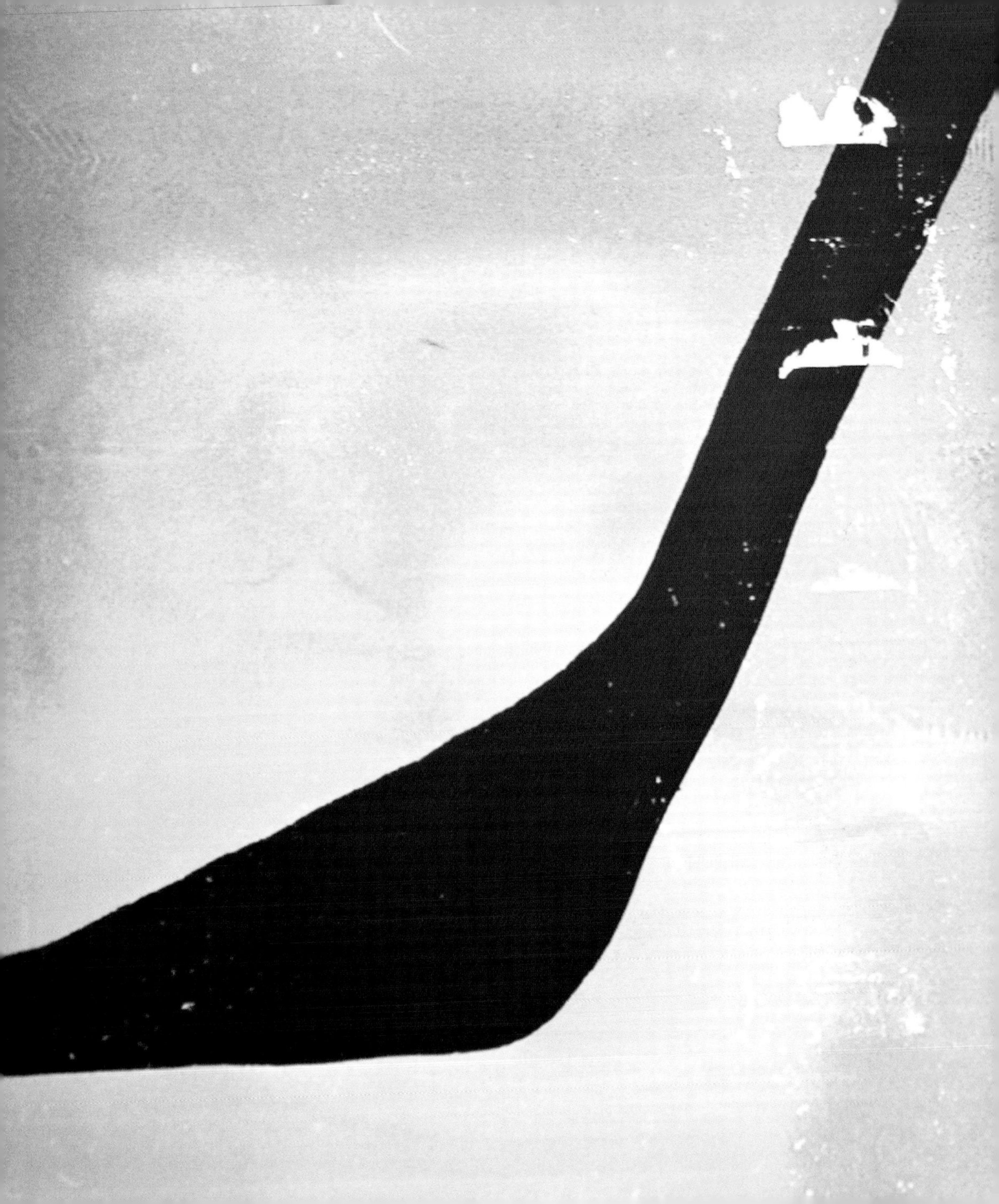

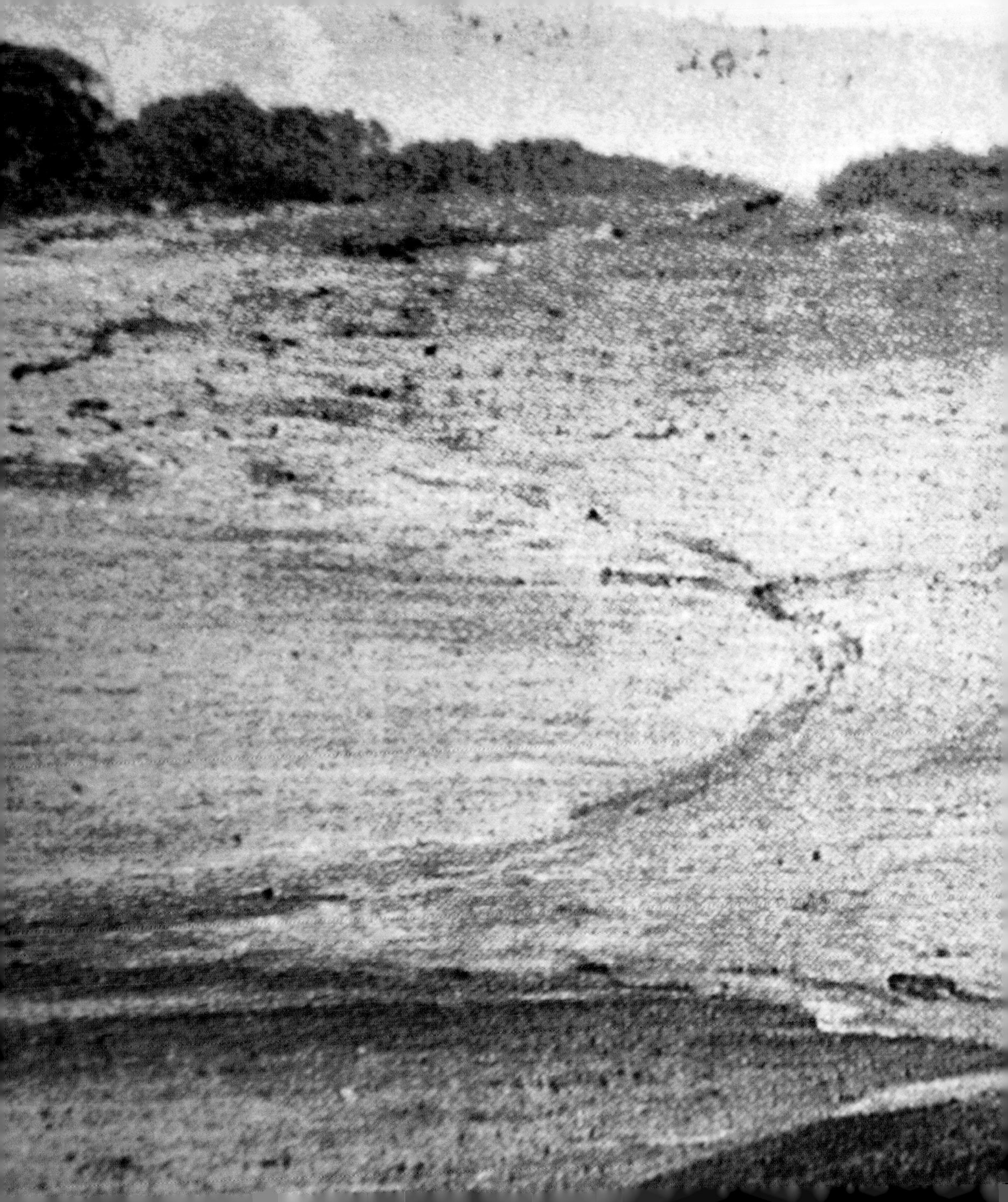

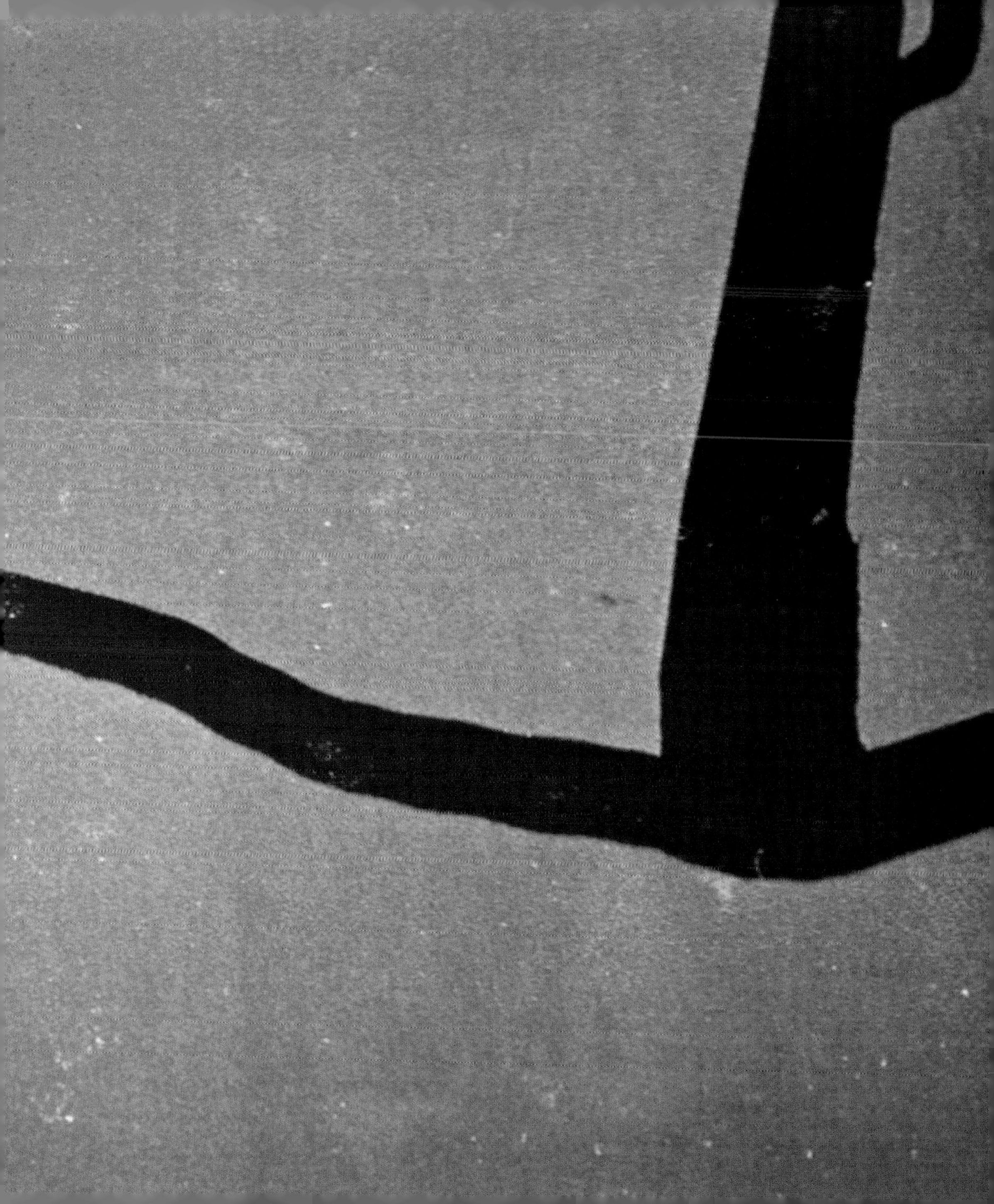

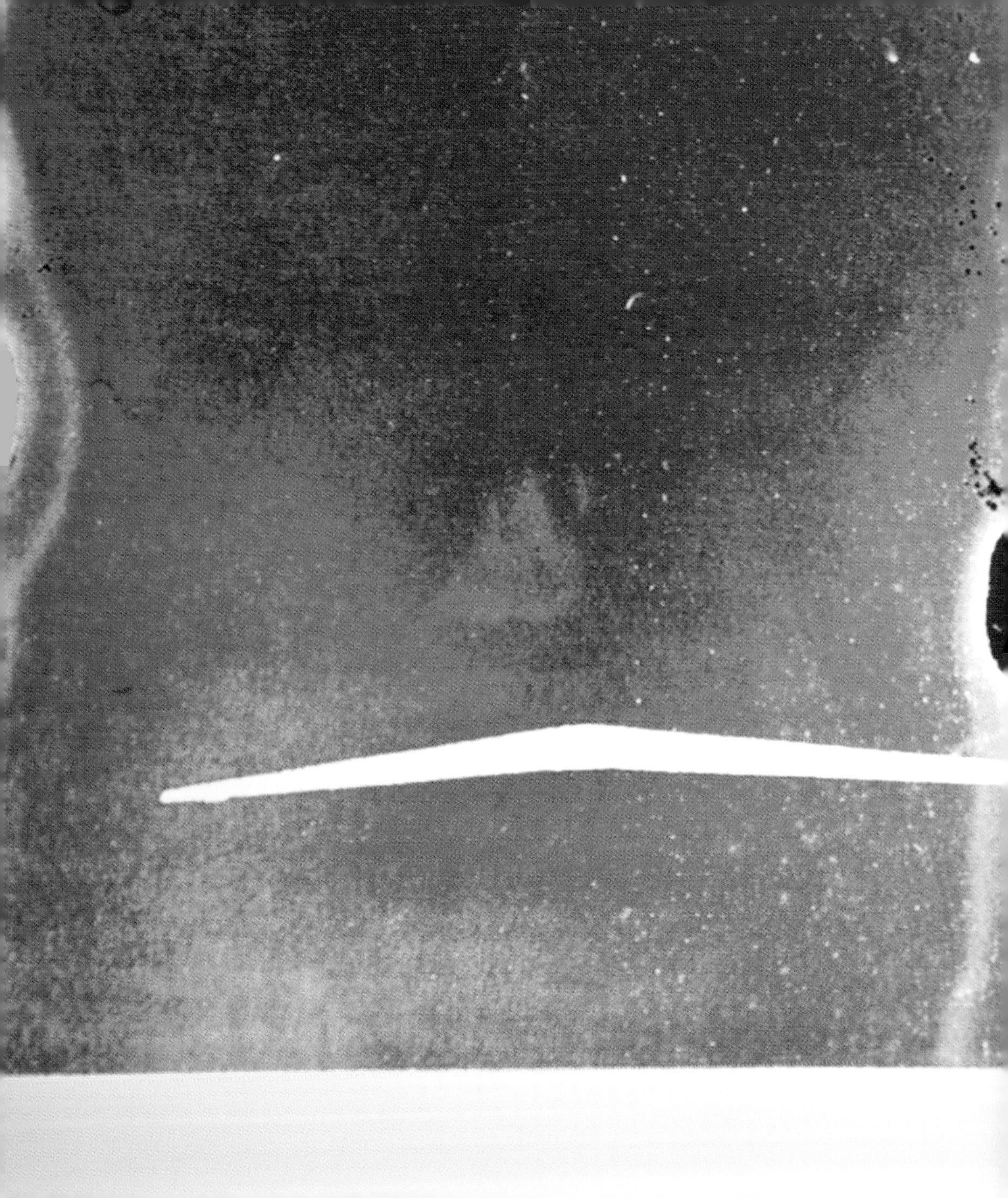

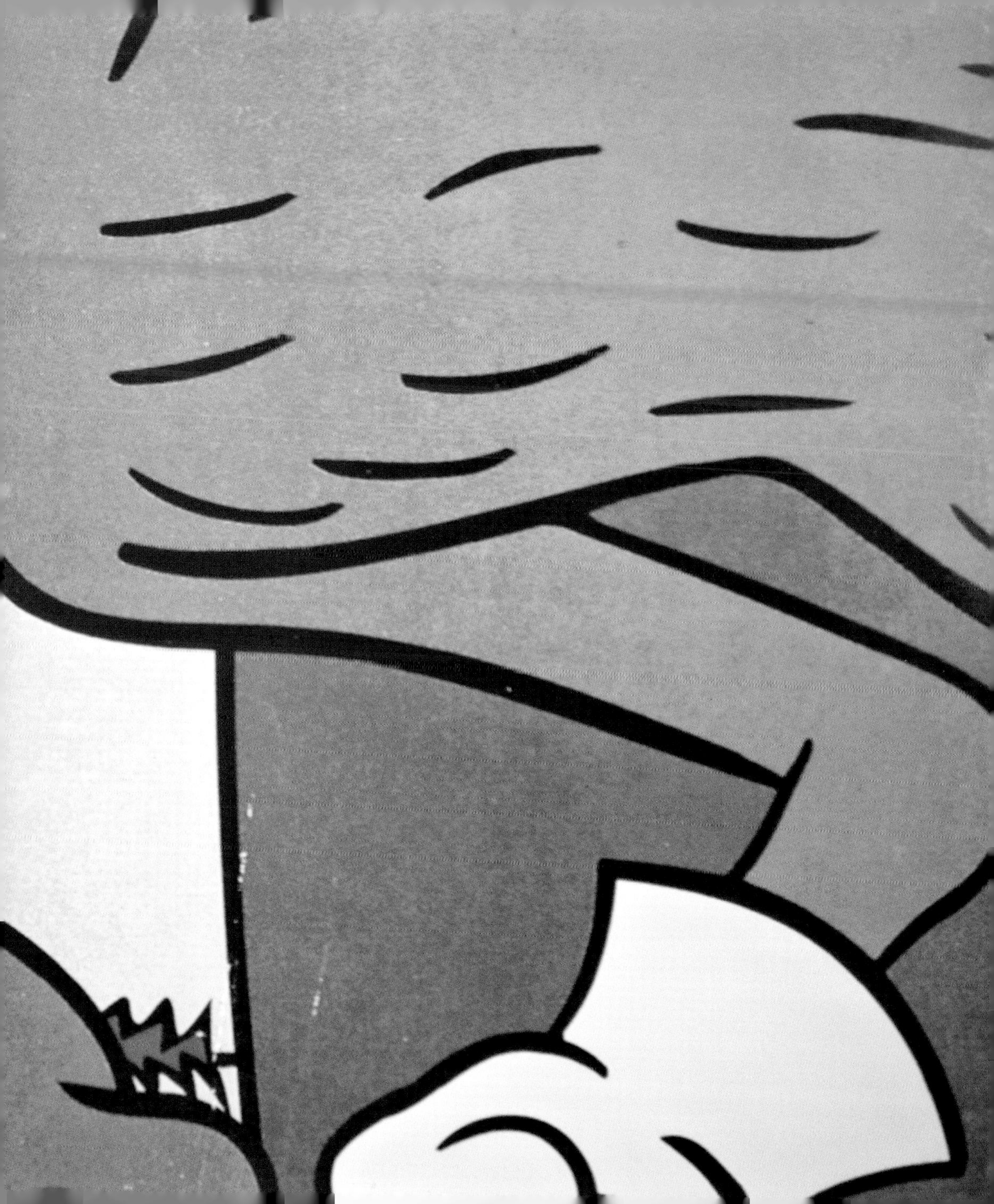

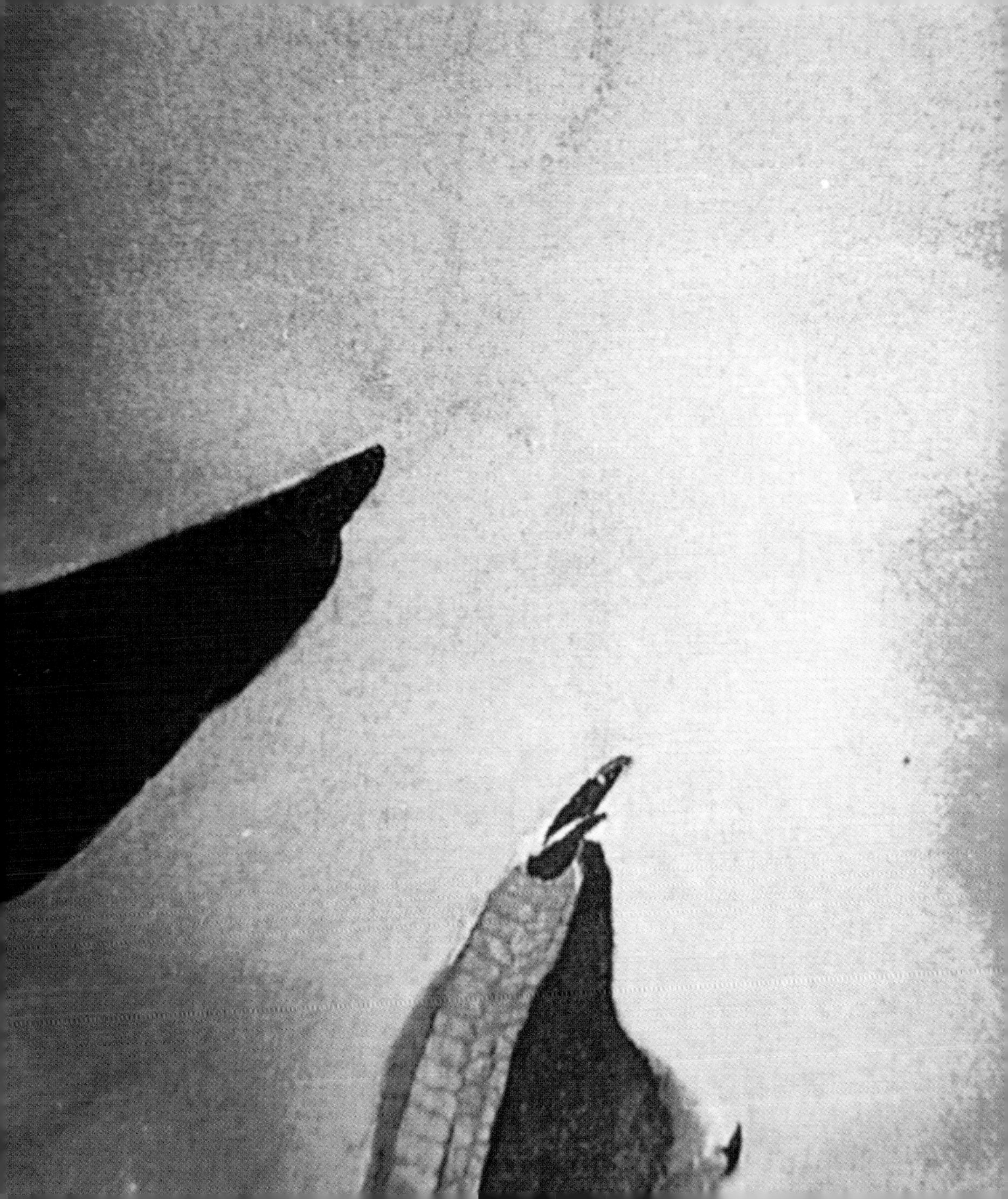

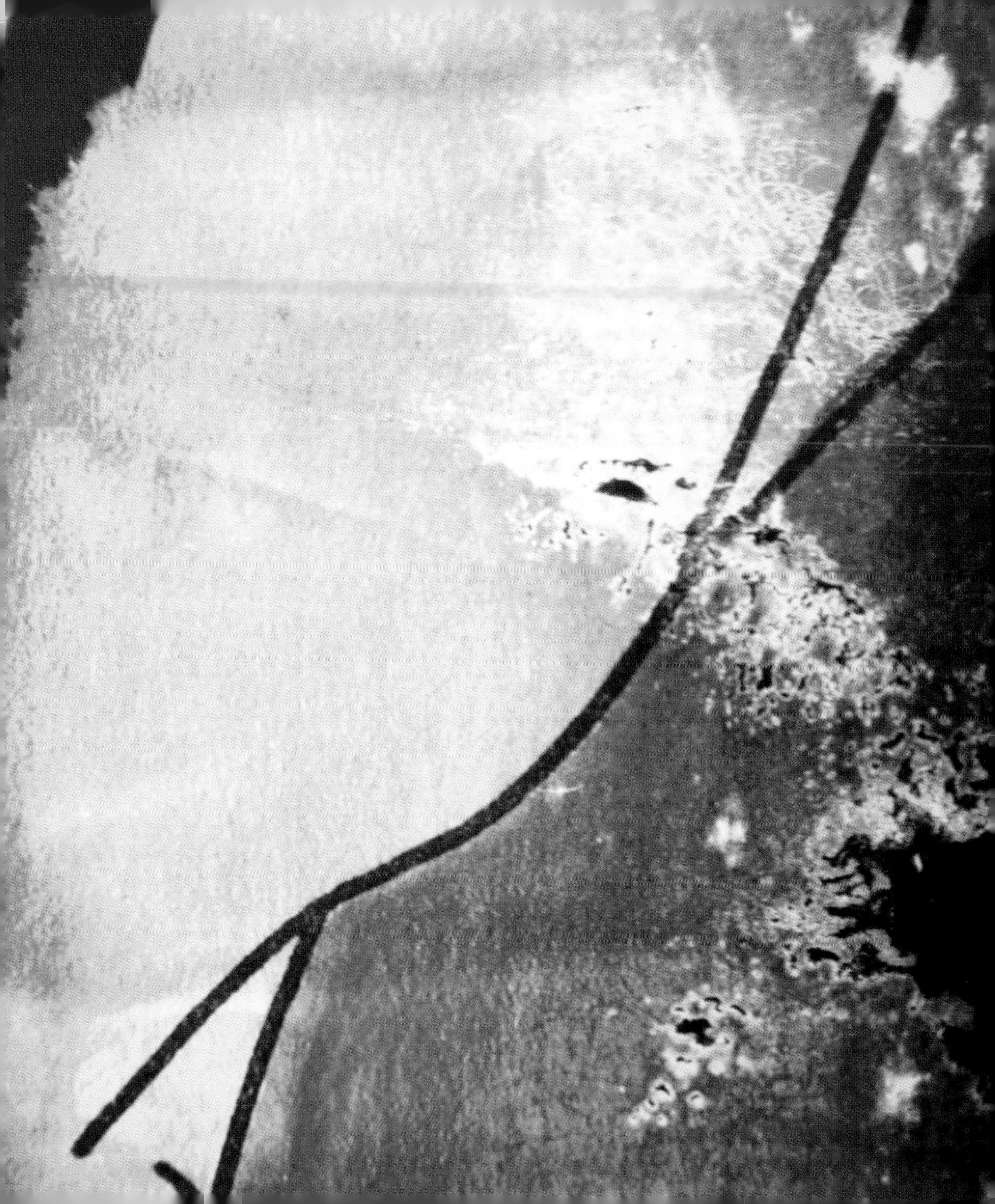

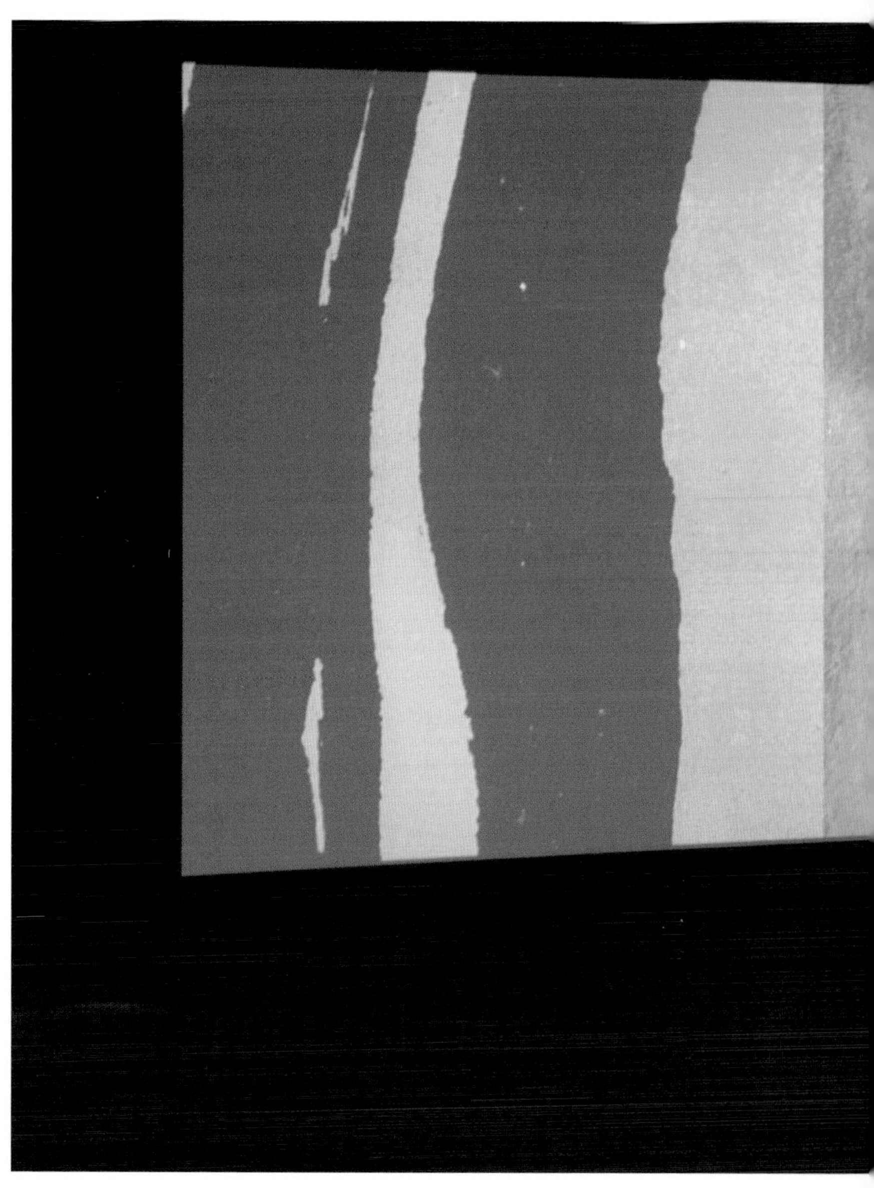

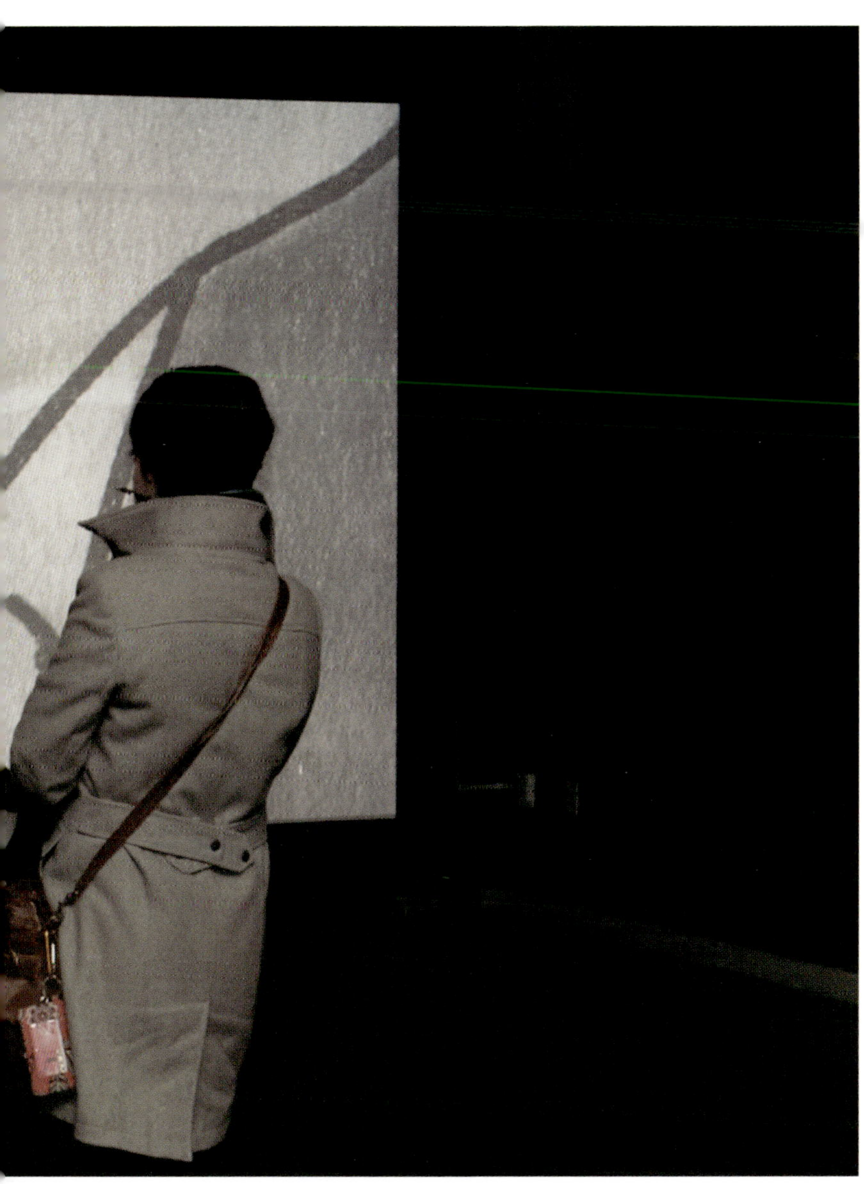

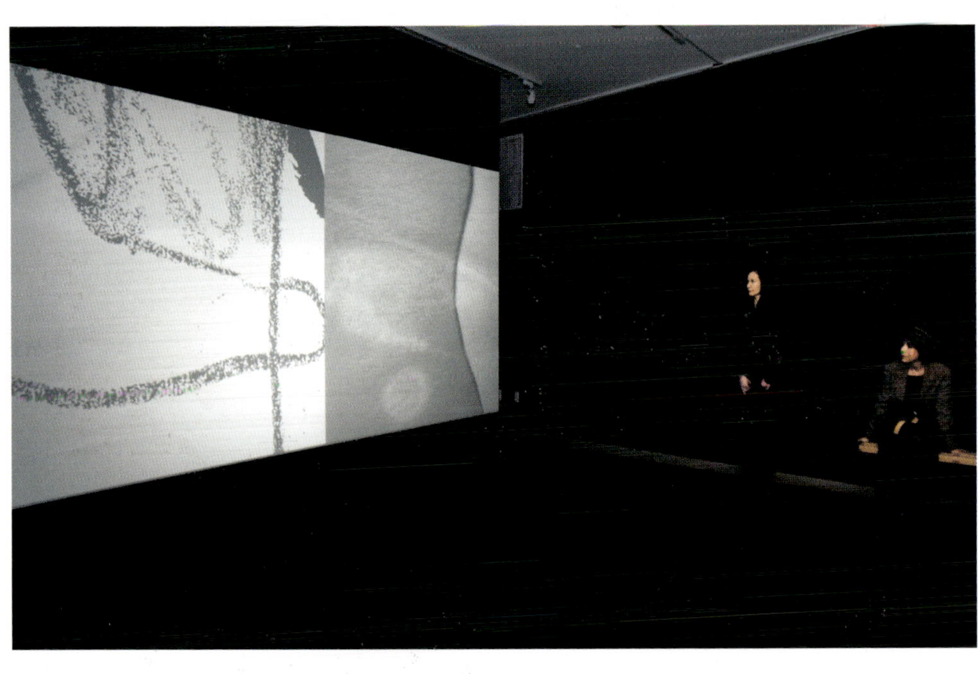

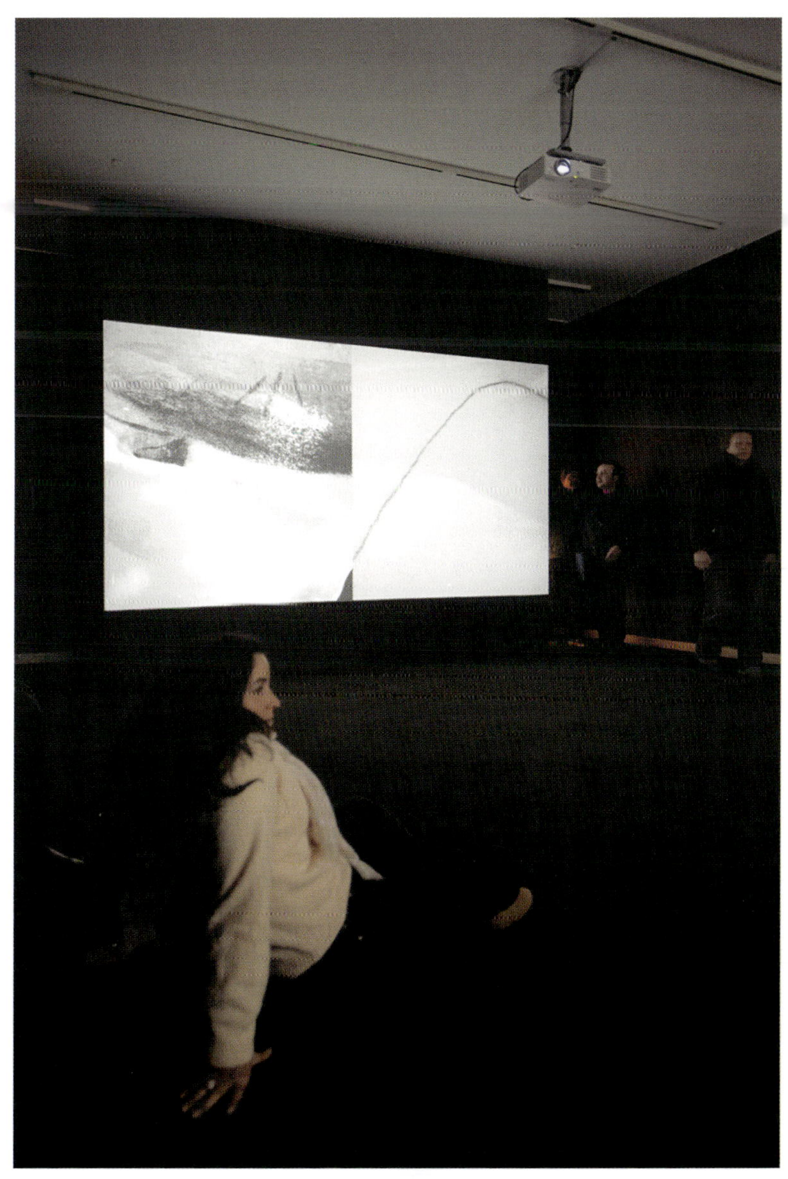

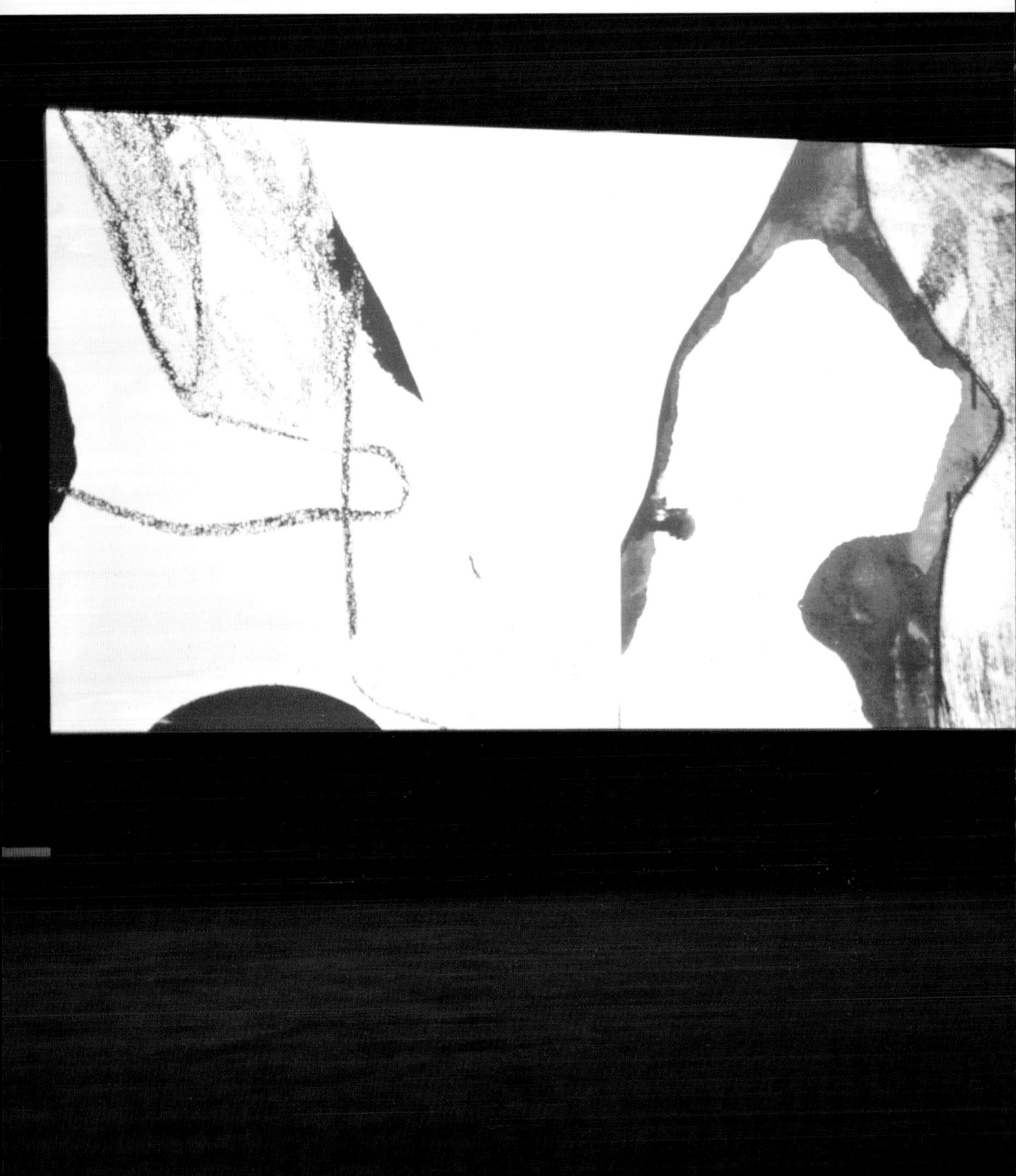

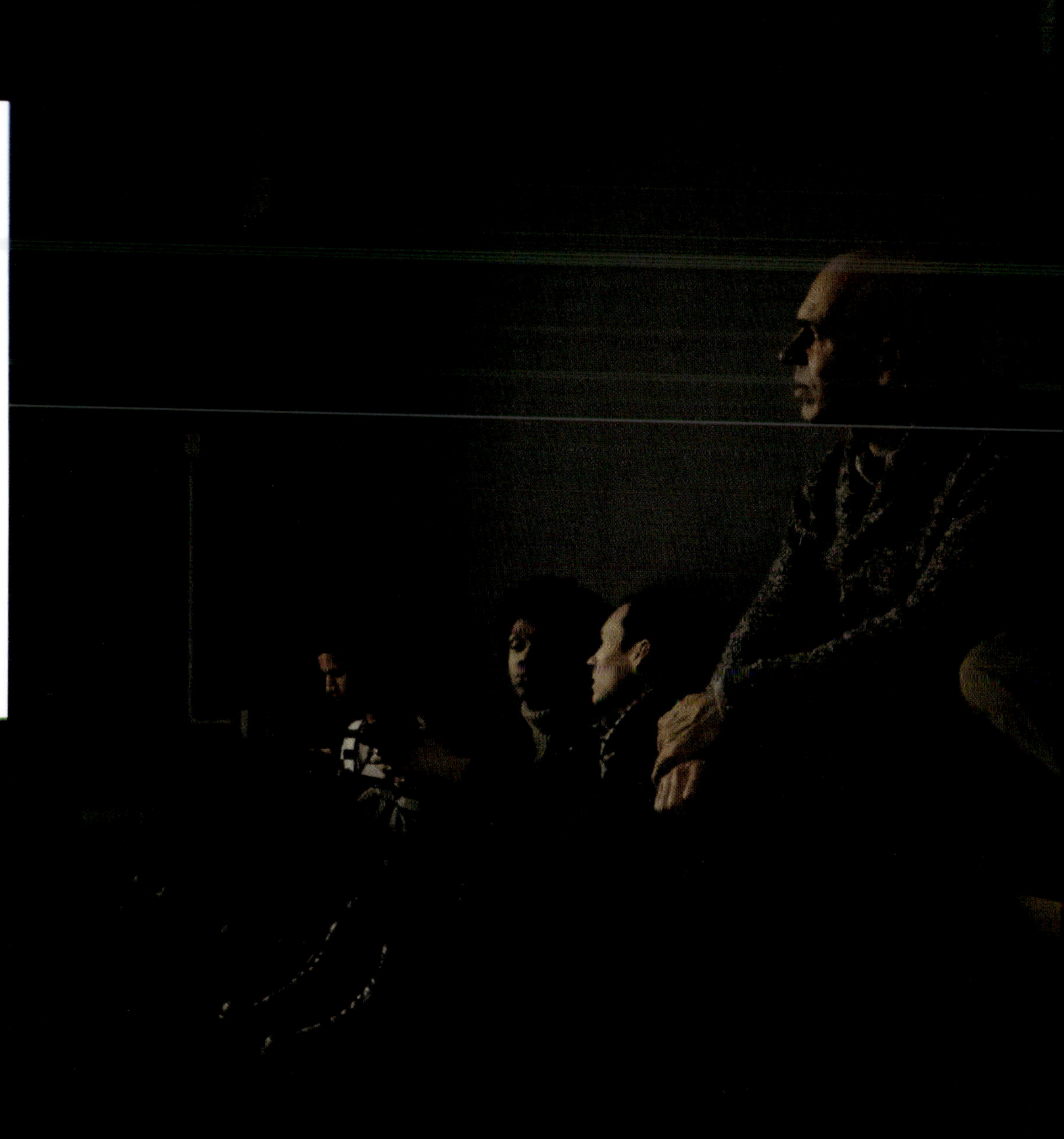

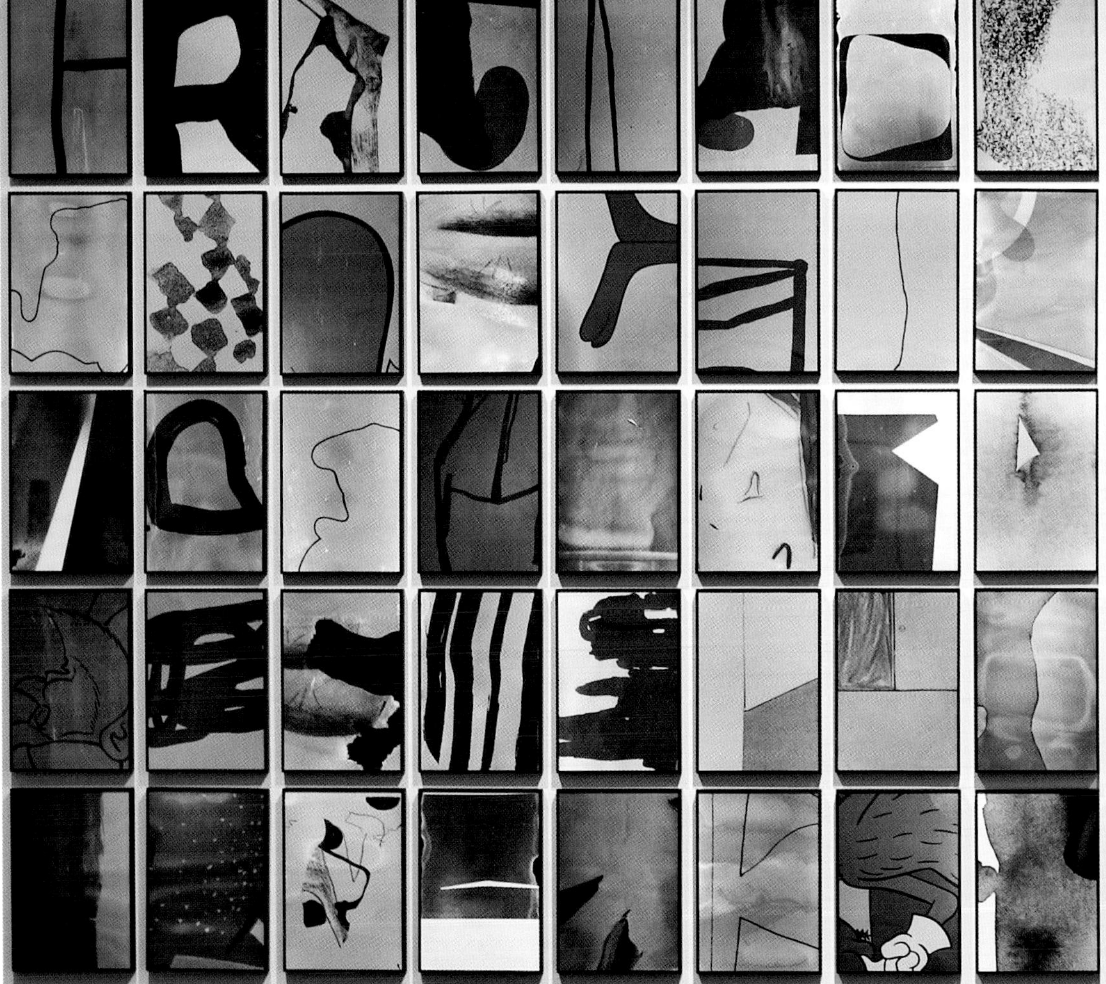

2. *Untitled*, 2004
Gelatin silver prints
80 parts, each 12 × 8 in.
La Colección Jumex, Mexico City

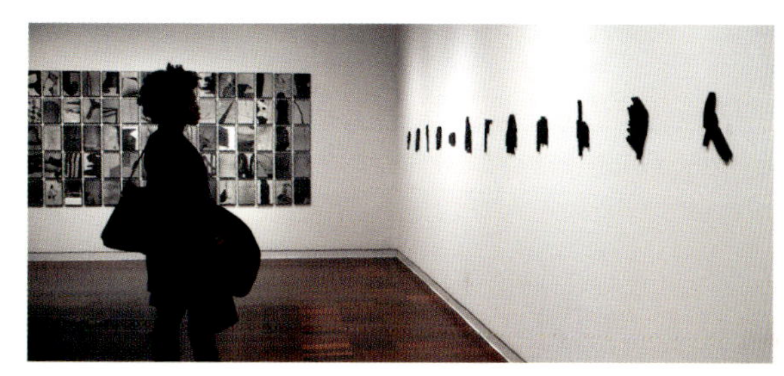

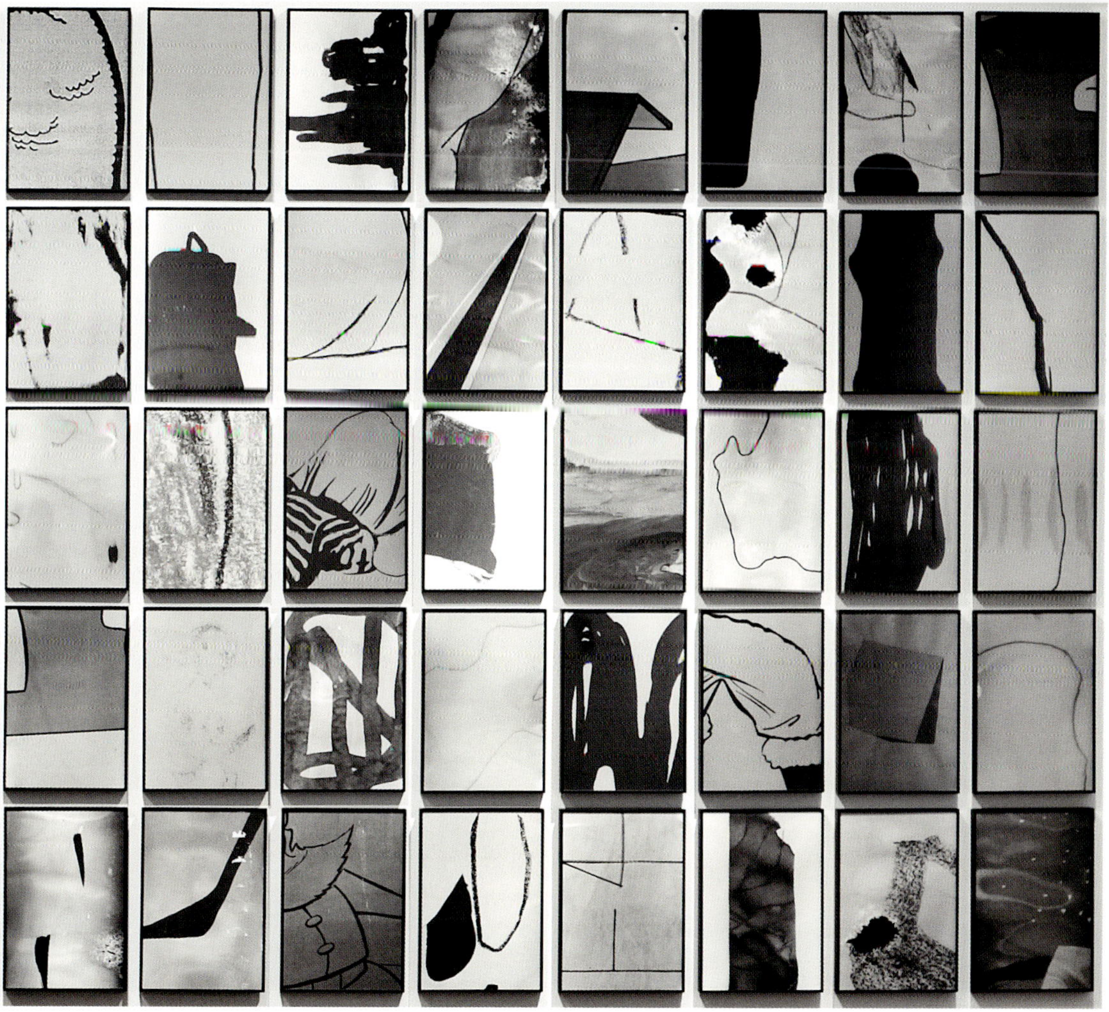

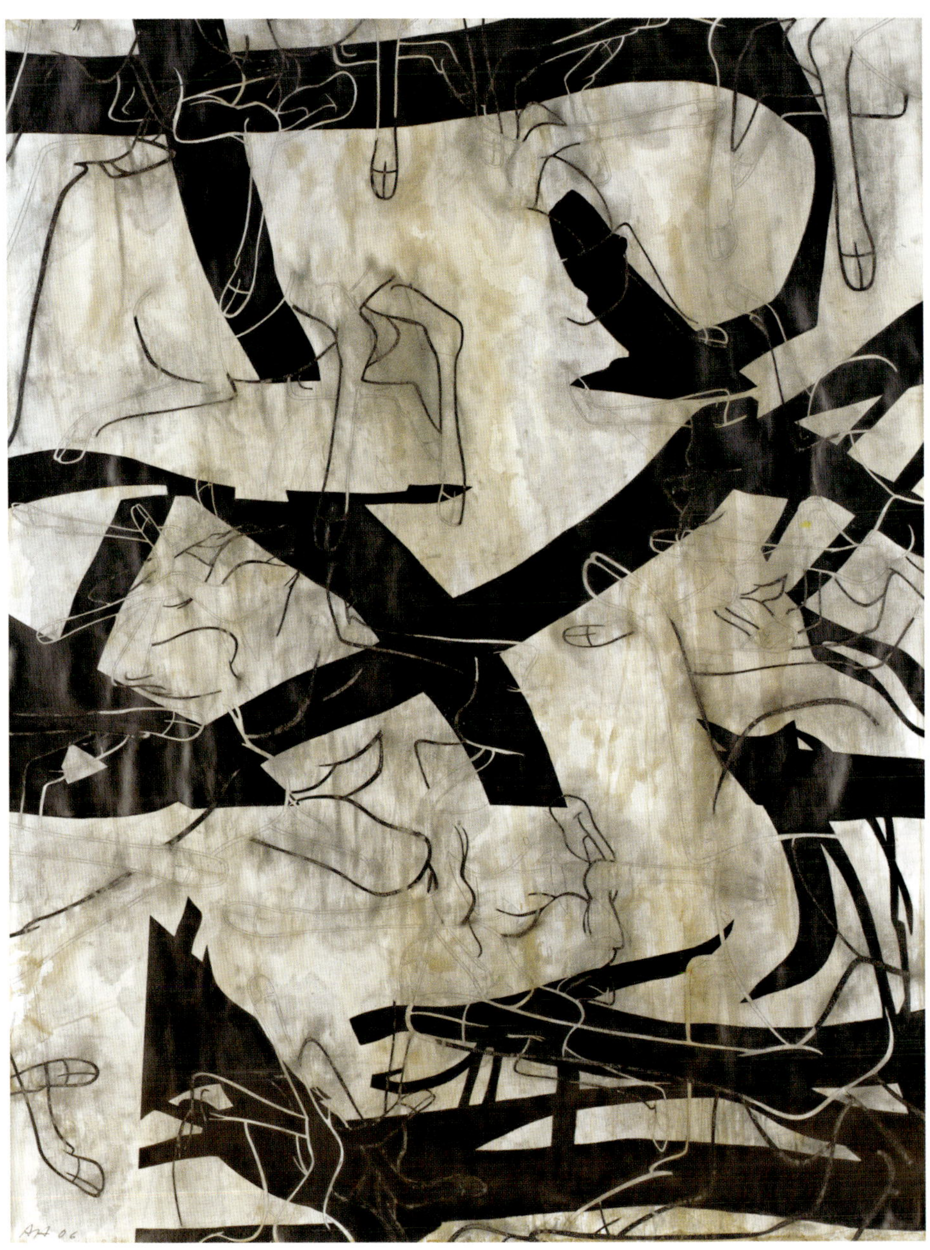

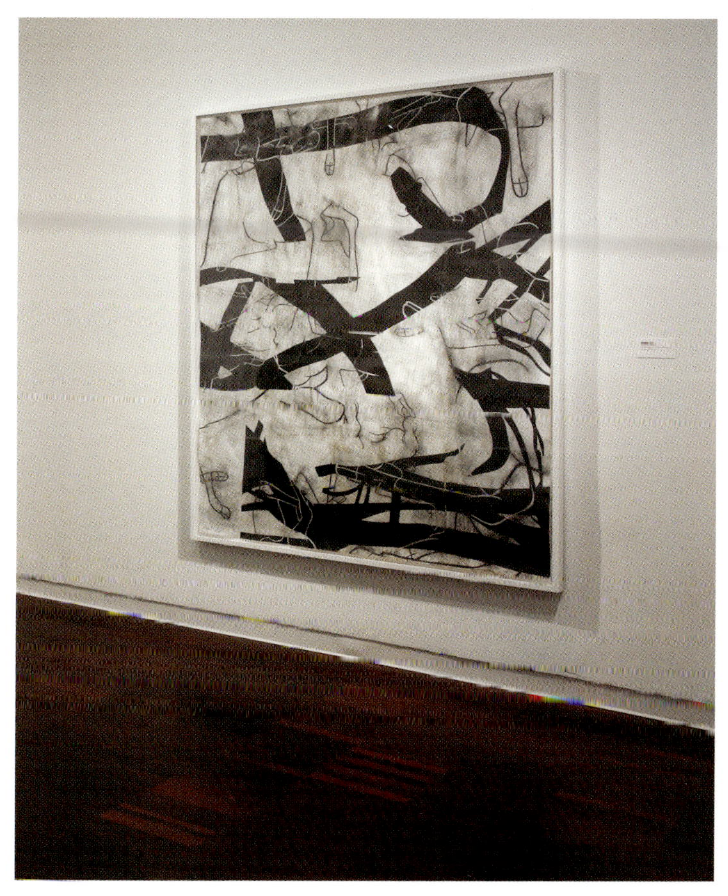

3. *Untitled*, 2006
Graphite and coffee on paper
80 × 58 in.
Collection Albright-Knox Art Gallery, Buffalo, NY
Gift of Deborah Ronnen, 2010

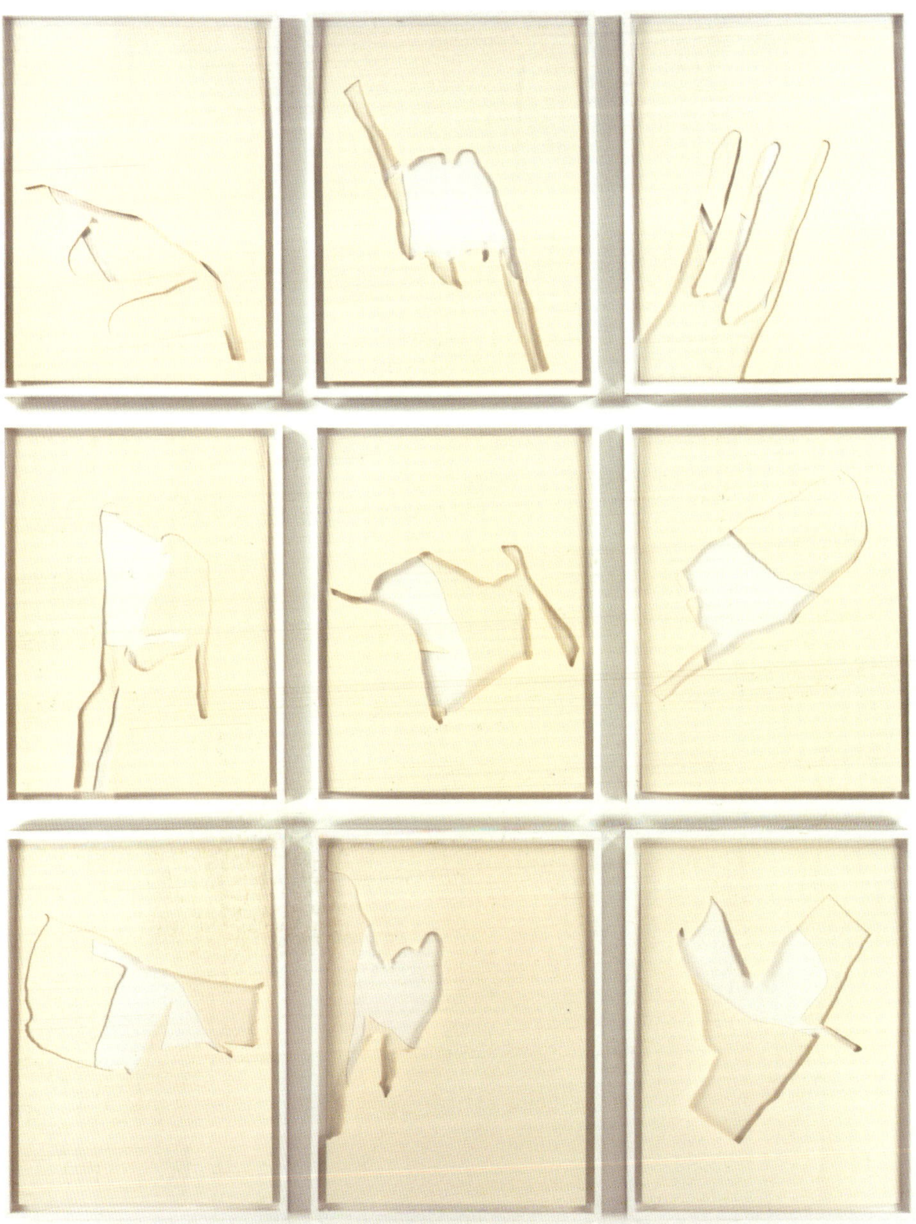

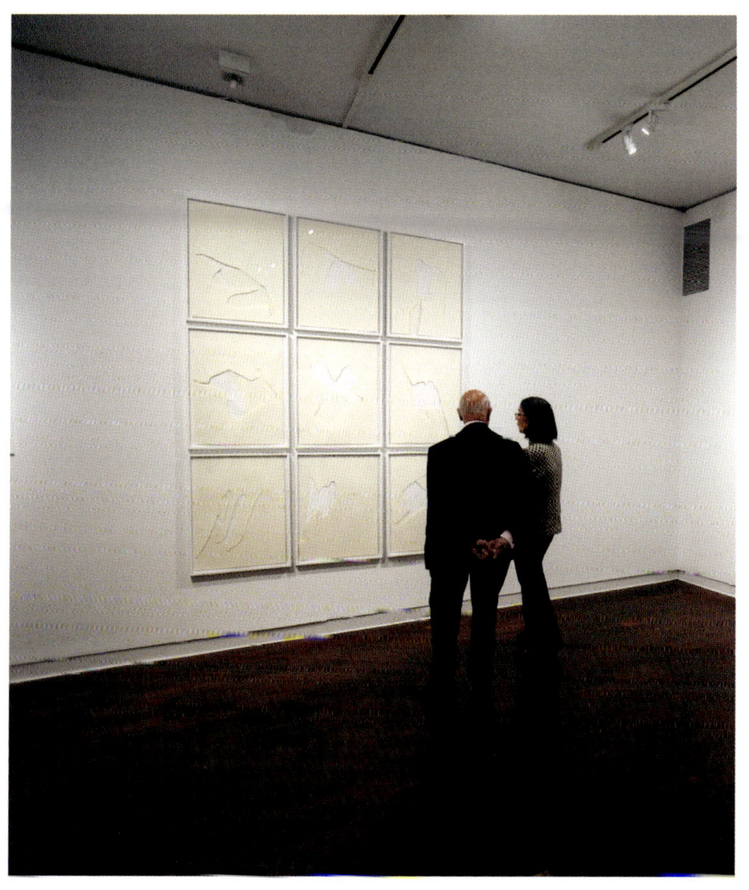

4. *From the Top (Cream)*, 2004
Cut paper
9 parts, each 27½ × 19¾ in.
Courtesy of the artist and Sikkema Jenkins & Co., NY

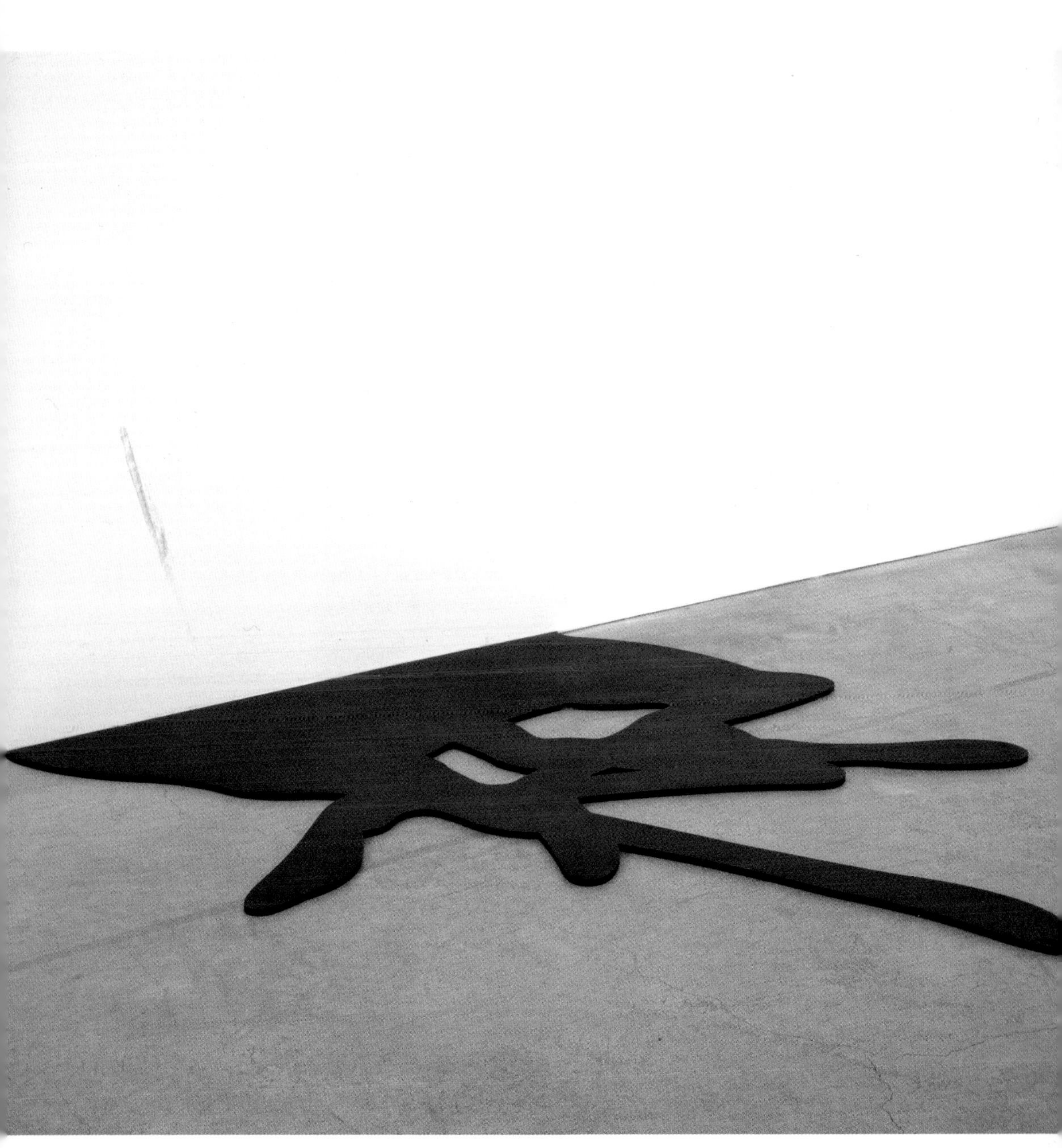

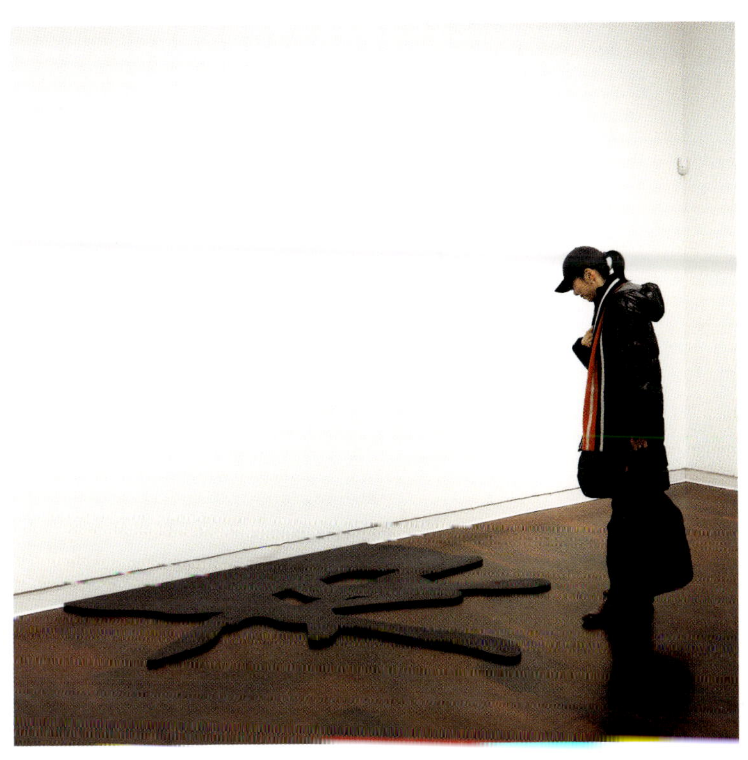

5. *Plot*, 2006
Steel
7/8 × 67 × 74 3/8 in.
Courtesy of the artist and Sikkema Jenkins & Co., NY

6. *Brinco*, 2007
Steel
$6\frac{5}{8} \times 11 \times \frac{3}{4}$ in.
Courtesy of the artist and Sikkema Jenkins & Co., NY

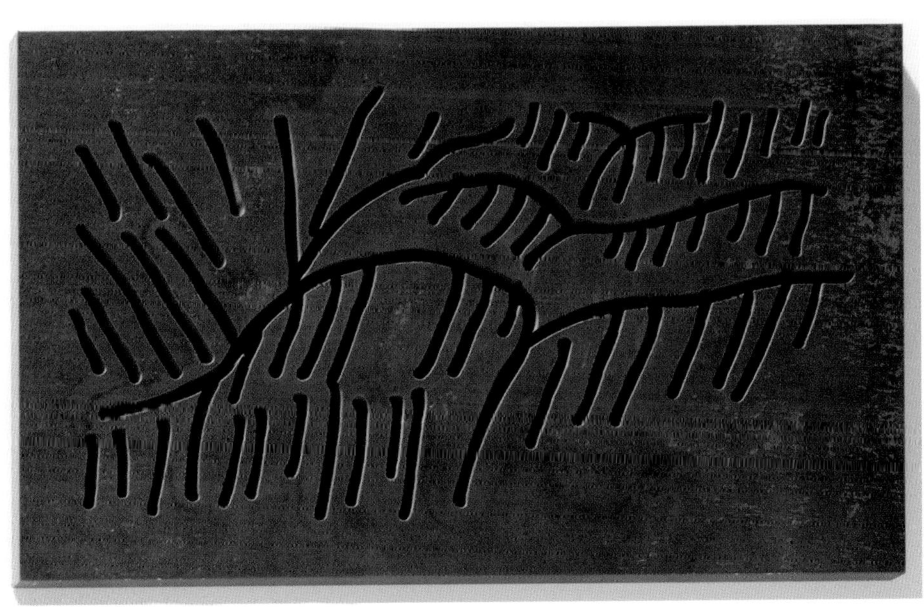

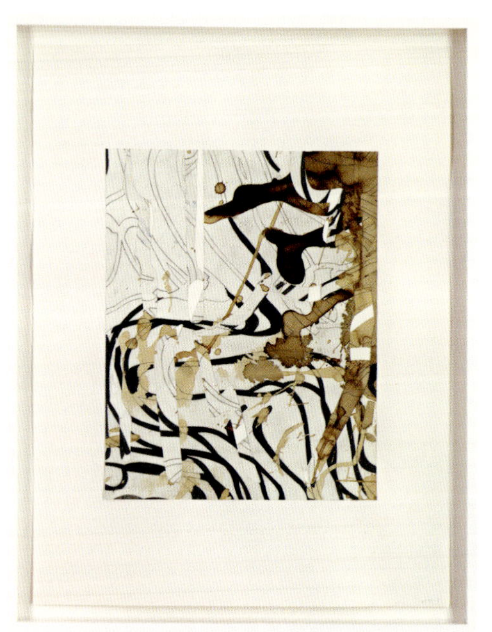

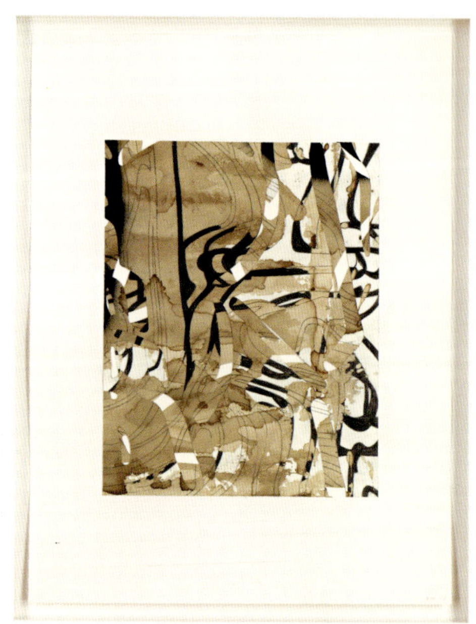

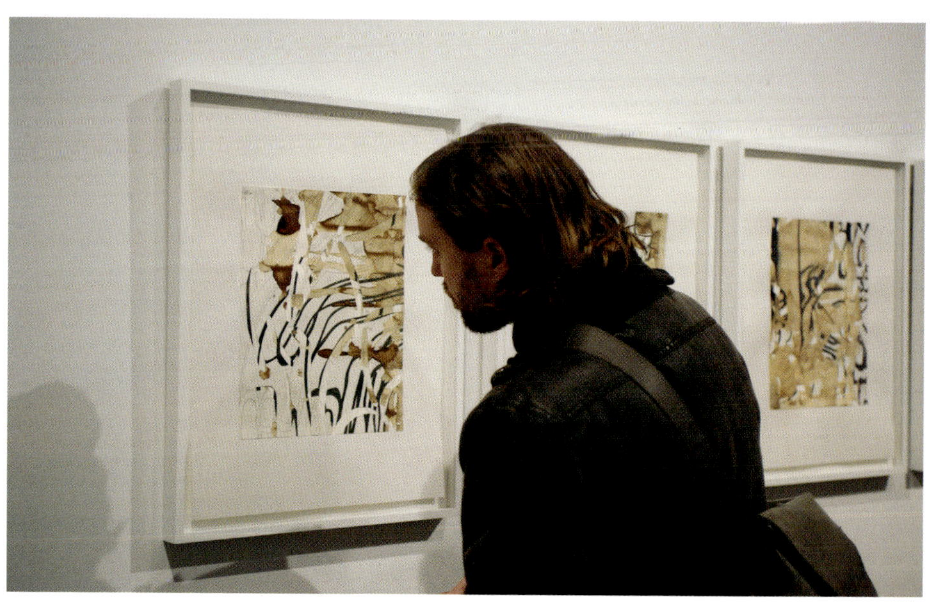

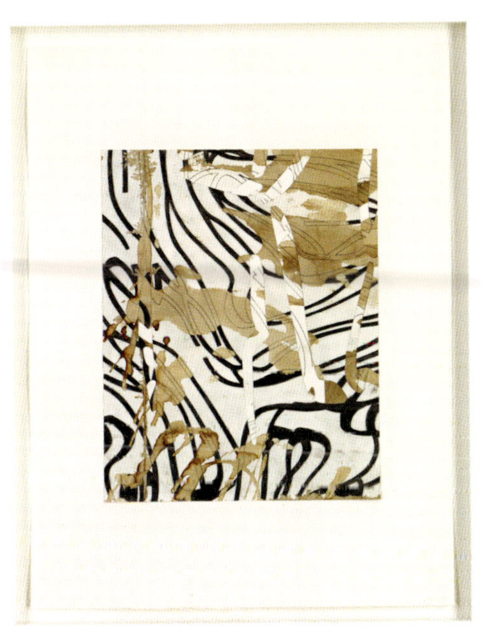

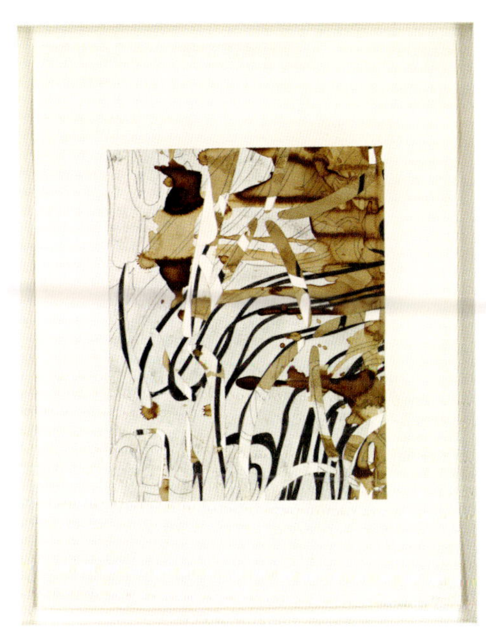

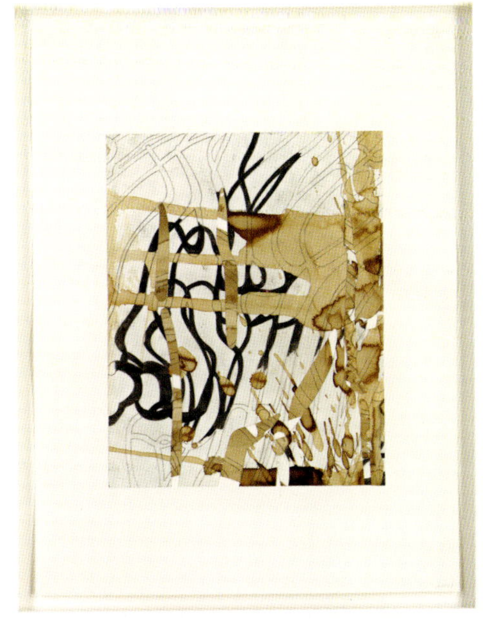

7. *Kugel*, 2008
Graphite, coffee, and paper on paper
5 parts, each 22⅛ × 16½ in.
Courtesy of Nicole Liarakos

8. *Walk*, 2009
Steel
14 parts, overall 11⅛ × approx. 115–20 in.
(length variable)
Courtesy of the artist and Sikkema Jenkins & Co., NY

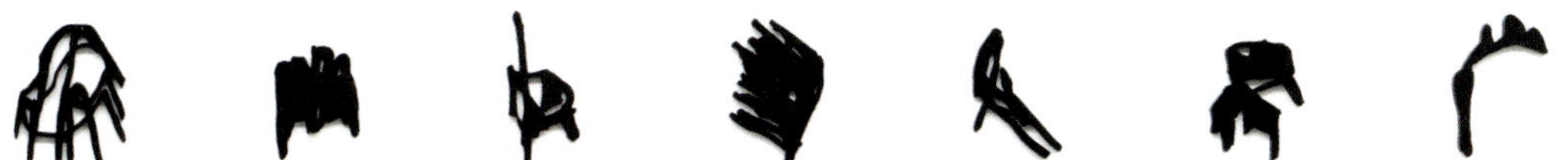

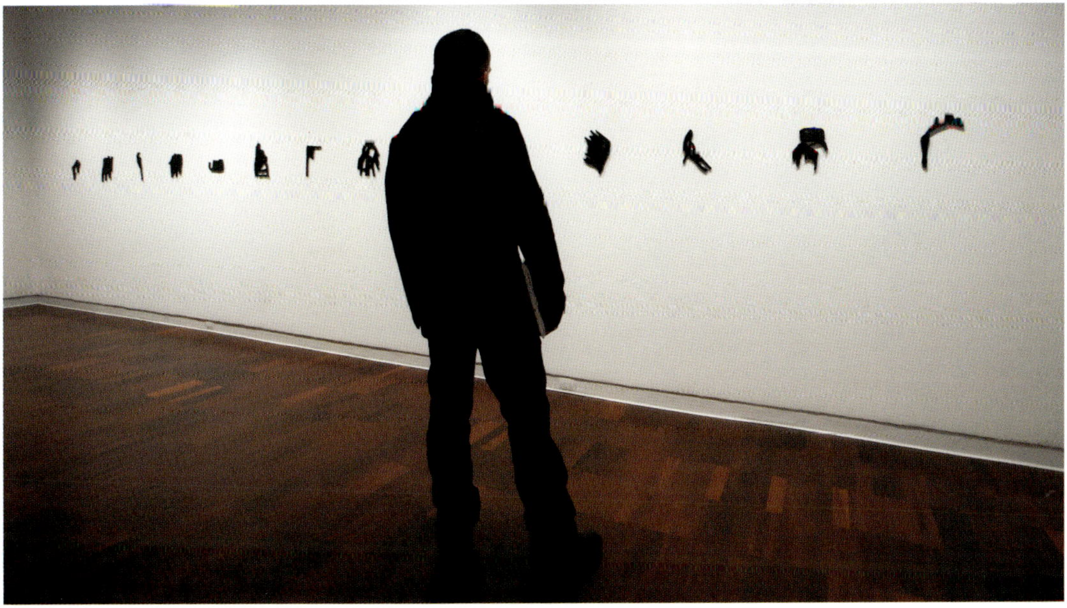

9. *Untitled*, 1992
Collage
4½ × 5⅞ in.
Collection of the artist, Berlin

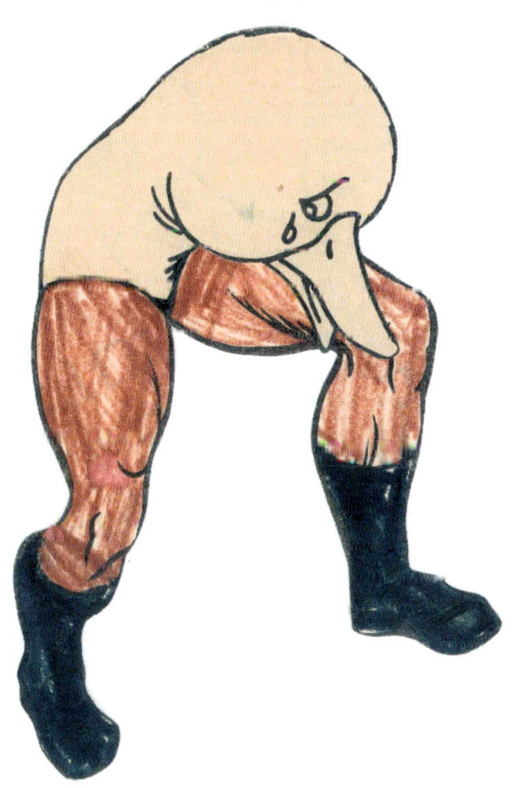

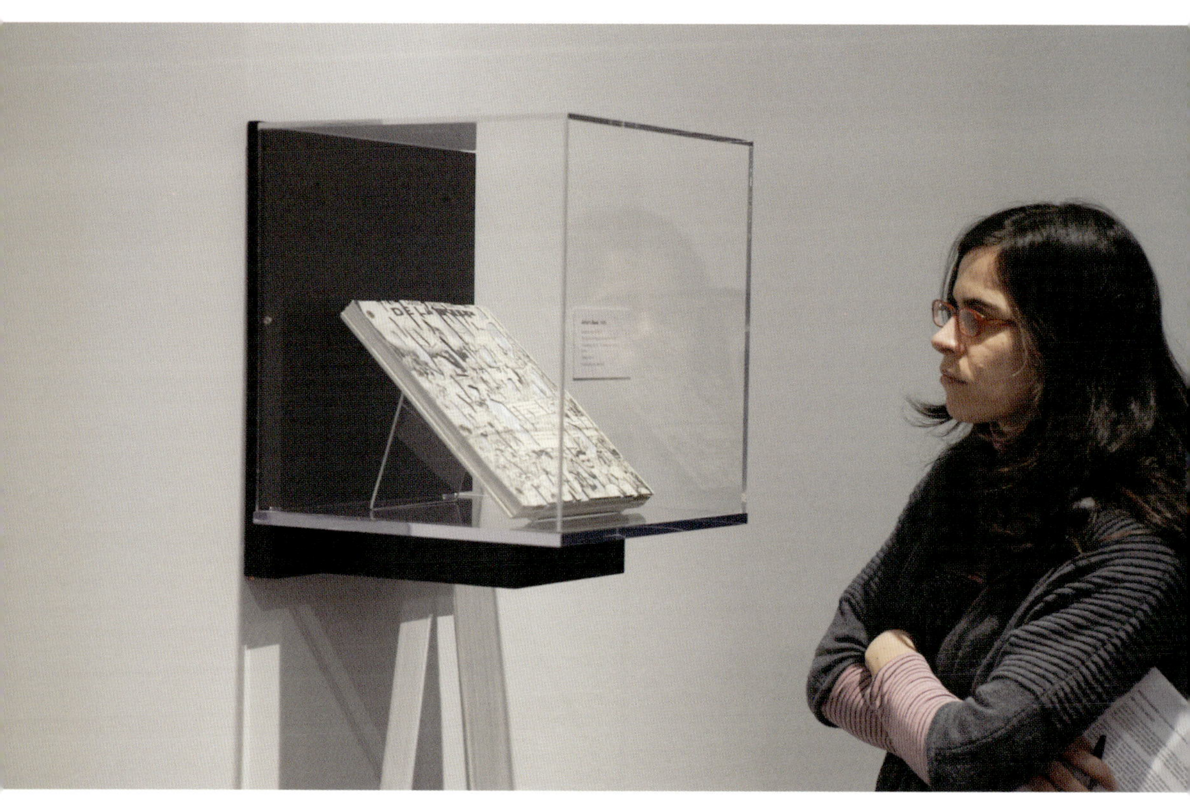

10. *Artist's Book*, 2009
Designed by Alvaro Sotillo
Texts by Miguel Miguel and Gabriela Rangel
Produced by Sala TAC–Trasnocho Arte Cultura, Caracas
Edition of 350
Private collection, New York

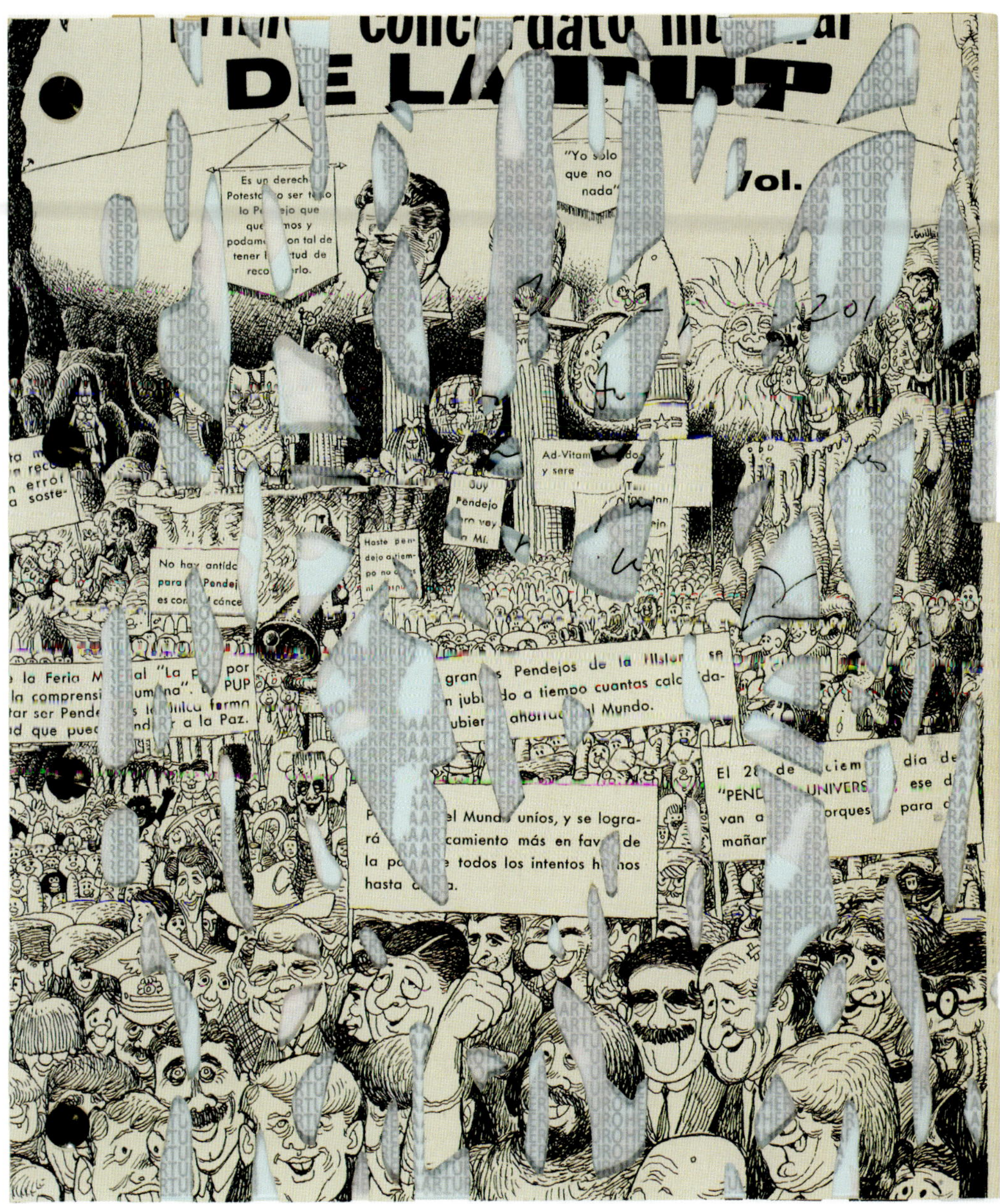
DE LA
Vol.
"Yo solo
que no
nada"
Es un derech
Ad-Vitam
y sere
Pendejo
No hay antídc
es con
e la Feria M
la comprensi
tar ser Pende
gran
s Pendejos de la
n jubi
do a tiempo cuantas calc
ubier
l Mundo.
El 28
van a
mañar
l Mundo unios, y se logra-
rá
camiento más en fav
de
la po
e todos los intentos h
nos
hasta

ARTIST'S BIOGRAPHY

Born 1959, Caracas, Venezuela
Lives and works in Berlin, Germany

EDUCATION

1992 MFA, University of Illinois at Chicago
1982 BFA, University of Tulsa, Oklahoma

SELECTED SOLO EXHIBITIONS & PROJECTS

2011 *Arturo Herrera: Les Noces* (The Wedding), Americas Society Art Gallery, New York, New York
Arturo Herrera, Sikkema Jenkins & Co., New York, New York

2010 *Home,* Haus am Waldsee, Berlin, Germany

2009 *Arturo Herrera,* Sala TAC: Trasnoche Arte Contacto, Caracas, Venezuela
Bitte Warten, Sox, Berlin, Germany

2007 *Arturo Herrera,* Ikon Gallery, Birmingham, and Kettle's Yard, Cambridge, United Kingdom
Arturo Herrera: Castles, Dwarfs, and Happychaps, The Aldrich Contemporary Art Museum, Ridgefield, Connecticut

2005 *Arturo Herrera,* Centro Galego de Arte Contemporánea, Santiago de Compostela, Spain
Getrennt, Aber Doch Zusammen, DAAD Galerie, Berlin, Germany

2002 *Present Tense No. 21: Arturo Herrera,* Art Gallery of Ontario, Toronto, Canada
ICA Ramp Project: You Go First, by Arturo Herrera, Institute of Contemporary Art, University of Pennsylvania, Philadelphia

2001 *Before We Leave,* Whitney Museum of American Art, New York, New York
Hammer Projects: Arturo Herrera, Hammer Museum, University of California, Los Angeles

2000 *Vertical Painting Series: Arturo Herrera: Party for Tom,* PS1 Contemporary Art Center, Long Island City, New York
Arturo Herrera, Centre d'Art Contemporain, Geneva, Switzerland

SELECTED GROUP EXHIBITIONS

2011 *Keep It Real: An Exhibition in Four Acts: Act 4: Material Intelligence,* Whitechapel Gallery, London, United Kingdom

2010 *On Line: Drawing Through the Twentieth Century,* The Museum of Modern Art, New York, New York
89 Km: Colección CGAC, MARCO: Museo de Arte Contemporánea de Vigo, Spain

2009 *Zeigen: An Audio Tour through Berlin,* Temporäre Kunsthalle, Berlin, Germany
7th Mercosul Biennial, Porto Alegre, Brazil
Forgotten Bar Project, Berlin, Germany
In a Room Anything Can Happen, CCS Bard Hessel Museum of Art, Bard College, Annandale-on-Hudson, New York
Compass in Hand: Selections from The Judith Rothschild Foundation Contemporary Drawings Collection, The Museum of Modern Art, New York, New York

2008 *La invención de lo cotidiano,* Acervos del Museo Nacional de Arte y de La Colección Jumex, Mexico City, Mexico
Order. Desire. Light. An Exhibition of Contemporary Drawings, Irish Museum of Modern Art, Dublin, Ireland
Prospect New Orleans: P1, New Orleans, Louisiana
Always There, Galerie Max Hetzler, Berlin, Germany
Adaptation, Smart Museum of Art, University of Chicago, Illinois

2007 *New Perspectives in Latin American Art, 1930–2006: Selections from a Decade of Acquisitions,* The Museum of Modern Art, New York, New York
Jump Cuts, Cisneros Fontanals Art Foundation, Miami, Florida
Comic Abstraction, The Museum of Modern Art, New York, New York

2006 *Anstoss Berlin,* Haus am Waldsee, Berlin, Germany
Transforming Chronologies: An Atlas of Drawings, Part Two, The Museum of Modern Art, New York, New York
Big Juicy Paintings (and More): Selections from the Permanent Collection, Miami Art Museum, Miami, Florida
Minimal, Galeria La Cuadra, Caracas, Venezuela
The New Collage, Pavel Zoubok Gallery, New York, New York

2005 *Drawing from The Modern, 1975–2005,* The Museum of Modern Art, New York, New York
Extreme Abstraction, Albright-Knox Art Gallery, Buffalo, New York
Exceeding Paint/Expanding Painting, Pratt Manhattan Gallery, New York, New York
Works on Paper, Galerie Max Hetzler, Berlin, Germany

ABOUT THE AUTHORS

NUIT BANAI

Nuit Banai received her Ph.D. in art history from Columbia University before joining the Department of Visual and Critical Studies at Tufts University/School of the Museum of Fine Arts, Boston. Specializing in postwar and contemporary art, Banai has written catalogue essays for major exhibitions at the Schirn Kunsthalle Frankfurt (2004), the Barbican Art Gallery, London (2005), and the Musée National d'Art Moderne–Centre Georges Pompidou, Paris (2006). Her essays and critical writings have appeared in publications for institutions such as Artists Space, the Bronx Museum of the Arts, and the Lower Manhattan Cultural Council in New York; the Museo d'Arte Moderna, Lugano, Switzerland; and the Bergen Kunsthalle, Norway, as well as the 3rd Singapore Biennial and Documenta 11. She recently finished a biography of Yves Klein for the *Critical Lives* series, which is scheduled for publication by Reaktion Books in 2011.

LYNN GARAFOLA

A dance historian and critic, Garafola is the author of *Diaghilev's Ballets Russes* (1998) and *Legacies of Twentieth-Century Dance* (2005), and she is the editor of several books, including *The Diaries of Marius Petipa* (which she also translated from the Russian; 1994), *Of, By, and For the People: Dancing on the Left in the 1930s* (1994), *José Limón: An Unfinished Memoir* (1998), and *The Ballets Russes and Its World* (1999). Curator of the New-York Historical Society's exhibition *Dance for a City: Fifty Years of the New York City Ballet* (1999) and the New York Public Library for the Performing Arts's *500 Years of Italian Dance: Treasures from the Cia Fornaroli Collection* (with Patrizia Veroli; 2007), as well as several smaller shows, she is a former Getty Scholar, a recipient of fellowships from the Social Science Research Council and the National Endowment for the Humanities, and a member of the American Academy of Arts and Sciences. Editor of the acclaimed series *Studies in Dance History,* she has also written for *Dance Magazine, The Nation, The Times Literary Supplement,* and many other publications. Most recently, she curated exhibitions on Jerome Robbins and on the Ballets Russes for the New York Public Library.

MONICA MASON

Trained at the Nesta Brooking School of Ballet and the Royal Ballet School, Mason joined the Royal Ballet in 1958, when she was only sixteen years old. She was appointed a soloist in 1963 and a principal in 1968, and she was highly praised for her interpretation of the leading role in Nijinska's *Les Noces.* In 1980 Mason was appointed Répétiteur to Kenneth MacMillan and, in 1984, Principal Répétiteur to the Royal Ballet. She went on to become Assistant Director in 1991 and Director in 2002. In July 1996, under the auspices of the Roehampton Institute, London, she was awarded an Honorary Doctorate by the University of Surrey. Mason was made an Officer of the Order of the British Empire in 2002, and on June 14, 2008, she was made a Dame of the British Empire.

CHRISTOPHER NEWTON

Trained in Leicestershire, Christopher Newton won a Leverhulme Trust Scholarship to study at the Royal Ballet School and joined the company in 1954. During the course of his long career, he danced a wide variety of roles, including that of the Rose Adagio Cavalier and that of the King in *The Sleeping Beauty;* that of Fencing Master in *A Rake's Progress;* that of Jason in *Sylvia;* and that of Concentration Commandant in *Valley of Shadows,* in addition to dancing the pas de trois in *Ballet Imperial* and roles in numerous other productions. In 1970 he went to San Diego to teach dance notation and repertory, returning to the Royal Ballet in 1973 when he was appointed first to the position of Notator, then to Répétiteur, and then, in 1988, to Ballet Master and Artistic Coordinator. He has mounted ballets for many other companies and staged his own production of *Swan Lake,* Act III, for the Pennsylvania Ballet. He retired from the Royal Ballet in 2001 and continues to work on a freelance basis.

GABRIELA RANGEL

Gabriela Rangel holds an M.A. in Curatorial Studies from the Center for Curatorial Studies at Bard College, an M.A. in Media and Communications Studies from the Universidad Católica Andrés Bello in Caracas, and a B.A. in Film Studies from the International Film School at San Antonio de los Baños, Cuba. She is currently the Director of Visual Arts and Chief Curator at the Americas Society. She was Assistant Curator of Latin American Art and Programs Coordinator for the International Center for the Arts of the Americas at the Museum of Fine Arts, Houston; curator and researcher at the Museo Alejandro Otero, Caracas; and curator at the Fundación Cinemateca Nacional, Caracas. She has curated a number of exhibitions on contemporary and modern art and has contributed to *Trans, Art Nexus,* and *Parkett.* Recent publications include *A Principality of Its Own: Forty Years of Visual Arts at the Americas Society* (Americas Society, New York, 2006), *SITAC VIII* (Patronato de Arte de Mexico, 2010–11), and *Marta Minujín: Minucodes* (Americas Society, New York, 2011). Her essays have appeared in *Da Adversidade Vivemos: Artistes d'Amerique Latine* (Musée d'Art Moderne de la Ville de Paris, 2001), *Liliana Porter* (Centro de Arte Recoleta, Buenos Aires, 2004), *Claudio Perna: Arte Social* (Galería de Arte Nacional, Caracas, 2004), *Arte no es Vida* (Museo del Barrio, New York, 2008), *Gordon Matta-Clark: Undoing Spaces* (Museu de Arte Moderna de São Paulo, 2010), and *Larger Than Life: Javier Téllez and Vasco Araujo* (Calouste Gulbenkian Foundation, Lisbon, 2010).

BIBLIOGRAPHY

Adams, Beverly. *Constructing a Poetic Universe: The Diane and Bruce Halle Collection of Latin American Art.* Houston: The Museum of Fine Arts, 2007.

________. *Contemporary Art and Latin America: Selections from the Diane and Bruce Halle Collection.* Tucson: Tucson Museum of Art, 2004.

Alexander, Randy. "Hero." *New Art Examiner* 23, no. 9 (May 1996): 54.

Apfelbaum, Polly and Marjorie Vecchio. *Whole Fragment.* Reno, NV: Sheppard Fine Arts Gallery and Black Rock Press, 2007.

Arratia, Euridice, Sabine Bartelsheim and Katja Blomberg. *Anstoss Berlin: Kunst macht Welt: Katalog zur Ausstellung im Haus am Waldsee.* Berlin: Haus am Waldsee, 2006.

Arturo Herrera: ruinas circulares. Caracas: Fundación D.O.P. / Odalys, 2009.

Bader, Graham. *Arturo Herrera: Boy and Dwarf.* Berlin: Holzwarth, 2007.

Barilli, Renato. *Officina America: Rete Emilia Romagna.* Milan: Mazzotta, 2002.

Basilio, Mariam, ed. *Latin American & Caribbean Art: MoMA at El Museo.* New York: El Museo del Barrio / Museum of Modern Art / D.A.P., 2004.

Baum, Kelly and Annette Carlozzi. *Blanton Museum of Art: American Art Since 1900.* Austin: University of Texas / Blanton Museum of Art, 2006.

Bauman, Zigmunt, Liam Gillick, Elisabeth Grosz, Boris Groys, Jackie Kay, Hanif Kureishi, Valerey Podoroga, Douglas Rushkoff, Carlos Varela, and Marina Warner. *Fresh Cream: Contemporary Art in Culture.* London: Phaidon, 2000.

Bechtel, Jeff and Wesley Miller. "Arturo Herrera: Assistant Jeff Bechtel." *Art:21 Blog* Video, August 7, 2009. http://blog.art21.org/2009/08/07/arturo-herrera-assistant-jeff-bechtel/.

Beck, Trisha and Kari Dahlgren, eds. *Life, Death, Love, Hate, Pleasure, Pain: Selected Works from the MCA Collection.* Chicago: Museum of Contemporary Art, Chicago, 2002.

Bell, Kirsty. *Works on Paper.* Berlin: Galerie Max Hetzler, 2005.

Bezzan, Cecilia and Daniel Cunin. *A Choice. A Snapshot of Contemporary Art, 14 Artists, 4 Curators, 9 Art Critics, 8 Venues on the Mont des Arts.* Brussels: Banque Bruxelles-Lambert, 2002.

Birbragher, Francine. "Body of Works." *ArtNexus* (April 1996): 105–7.

Block, Holly. *All About Paint.* Memphis: Art Museum of the University of Memphis, 2001.

Bloemink, Barbara and Vicky A. Clark. *Comic Release: Negotiating Identity for a New Generation*. New York: D.A.P., 2003.

Blomberg, Katja. *Arturo Herrera: Home*. Cologne: W. König, 2010.

Borchardt-Hume, Achim. *Keeping it Real: From the Ready-made to the Everyday, the D. Daskalopoulos Collection*. London: Whitechapel Gallery, 2011.

Boris, Staci. *Drawing on the Figure: Works on Paper of the 1990s from the Manilow Collection*. Chicago: Museum of Contemporary Art, 2000.

Bradley, Jessica. *Fragments and Figments: Arturo Herrera Works on Paper, January 30–April 28, 2002*. Toronto: Art Gallery of Toronto / Musée des beaux-arts de l'Ontario, 2002.

Briggs, Patricia. "Painting at the Edge of the World." *Artforum* 39, no. 10 (Summer 2001): 185–86.

Brodsky, Seth, Anthony Elms, Darby English, Josiah McElheny, and Diane Williams. *Arturo Herrera and David Schutter*. Chicago: Tony Wight Gallery, 2010.

Butler, Cornelia and Catherine de Zegher. *On Line: Drawing Through the Twentieth Century*. New York: Museum of Modern Art, 2010.

Camper, Fred. "Arturo Herrera at the Renaissance Society." *Chicago Reader*, February 13, 1998, pp. 28–29.

Caniglia, Julie. "Arturo Herrera." *Artforum* 39, no. 5 (January 2001): 138.

Cassel, Valerie, Roger Sabin and Bernard Welt. *Splat, Boom, Pow! The Influence of Cartoons in Contemporary Art*. Houston: Contemporary Arts Museum, 2003.

Christofori, Ralf. *Arturo Herrera: Photographs*. New York and Torino: Sikkema Jenkins / Galleria Franco Noero, 2005.

__________. *Goofy's Hermeneutic Crisis, Color Me Blind!* Stuttgart: Württembergischer Kunstverein, 1999.

Christov-Bakargiev, Carolyn. *Arturo Herrera*. Los Angeles: UCLA Hammer Museum of Art and Cultural Center, 2001.

Cohen, David. "Yours Until the Walls Come Down." *New York Sun*, August 10, 2006.

Cotter, Holland. "The Joys of Childhood Reexamined." *New York Times*, March 25, 1994, p. 30.

Dexter, Emma. *Vitamin D: New Perspectives in Drawing*. New York: Phaidon, 2005.

Estep, Jan. "Arturo Herrera." *New Art Examiner* 25, no. 6 (March 1998): 50–51.

Falcón, Dubraska. "Todos quieren a Arturo Herrera." *El Universal*, June 18, 2009.

Fernandez-Cid, Miguel, ed. *Arturo Herrera: Keep in Touch = En contacto.* Santiago de Compostela: Centro Galego de Arte Contemporánea / Xunta de Galicia, 2005.

Firstenberg, Lauri, Douglas Fogle and Peter Pakesh. "Curating Painting." *Flash Art* (November–December 2002): 59–61.

Fitzpatrick, Robert, Pearlman, Alison, Julie Rodrigues Widholm, and Elizabeth A. T. Smith. *Life, Death, Love, Hate, Pleasure, Pain: Selected Works from the Museum of Contemporary Art, Chicago, Collection.* Chicago: Museum of Contemporary Art, 2002.

Fogle, Douglas. *Painting at the Edge of the World.* Minneapolis: Walker Art Center, 2001.

Gamerro, Carlos, Rubén Mira, Victoria Noorthoorn, and Alejandro Tantian. *La 11e Biennale de Lyon: Une terrible beauté est née.* Les Presses du Réel, 2011.

Gioni, Massimiliano. "Painting at the Edge of the World." *Flash Art* (May–June 2001): 147.

Gobin, Gilbert. "Promenade d'art contemporain au Coeur du Mont des Arts." *L'Echo,* October 10, 2002.

Gómez, Dulce and Francisco Villanueva y Madrid. *Arte contemporáneo de Venezuela = Contemporary Art of Venezuela.* Caracas: Francisco Villanueva, 2006.

Grabner, Michelle. "Arturo Herrera, Renaissance Society & Wooster Gardens." *Art Press* 234, no. 80 (April 1998): 80–81.

________. "Painting at the Edge of the World." *Freize* 60 (June–August 2001): 116–17.

Grachos, Louis, Claire Schneider and Pae White. *Extreme Abstraction.* Buffalo: Albright-Knox Gallery, 2005.

Hainley, Bruce and John Slyce. *The Americans: New Art.* London: Barbican Gallery / Booth-Clibborn, 2001.

Hammer Projects, 1999–2009. Los Angeles and New York: Hammer Museum and D.A.P., 2009.

Heartney, Eleanor. *GSA Art in Architecture: Selected Artworks, 1997–2008.* Washington, D.C.: General Services Administration, Public Buildings Service, 2008.

Helguera, Pablo. "Arturo Herrera, The Edges of the Invisible." *ArtNexus* 33 (August–October 1999): 48–52.

________. "Imaginary Landscape." *Tema Celeste* 83 (January–February 2001): 46–51.

Henry, Claude. "Quatorze artistes contemporains à Bruxelles, grâce à la BBL." *Banque Active,* September 16, 2002.

Herrera, Arturo and Jonathan Munar. "Arturo Herrera: Music." *Art:21 Blog* Video, May 7, 2009. http://blog.art21.org/2009/05/07/arturo-herrera-music/.

Herrera, Arturo and Jonathan Munar. "Arturo Herrera: Powerful Images." *Art:21 Blog* Video, June 19, 2009. http://blog.art21.org/2009/06/19/arturo-herrera-powerful-images/.

Herrera, Arturo and Jonathan Munar. "Arturo Herrera: Failure." *Art:21 Blog* Video, September 25, 2009. http://blog.art21.org/2009/09/25/arturo-herrera-failure/.

Herrera, Arturo and Stephanie Smith. "Interview." Chicago: Smart Museum of Art, 2008. http://adaptation.uchicago.edu/artists/herrera/interview/

Hixon, Kathryn. "Clarity." *New Art Examiner* 23, no. 9 (May 1996): 42–43.

________. "Arturo Herrera at Randolph Street Gallery." *Flash Art* (October 1995): 111.

Hobbs, Robert. *In Context: Collage + Abstraction.* New York: Pavel Zoubok Gallery, 2002.

Holzwarth, Hans Werner. *Art Now. A Cutting Edge Selection of Today's Most Exciting Artists.* Vol. 3. London: Taschen, 2008.

Iles, Chrissie, Christianne Paul, Lawrence Rinder, and Debra Singer. *2002 Biennial Exhibition.* New York: Whitney Museum of American Art, 2002.

Inboden, Gudrun. *Always There.* Berlin: Galerie Max Hetzler, 2008.

Jacobson, Marjory. "On Arturo Herrera at the ARCO '01 Fair." *Revista ARCO '01* (2001).

Jarton, Cyril, Ronald van de Sompel, Narcisse Tordoir, Luc Tuymans, Kurt Vanbelleghem, and Tim Vermeulen. *Trouble Spot: Painting.* Antwerp: NICC / MUHKA, 1999.

Johnson, Ken. "Market-Driven Survey Through the 20th Century." *New York Times,* February 21, 2003, p. 42.

Juncosa, Enrique, ed. *Order, Desire, Light: An Exhibition of Contemporary Drawing.* Dublin: Irish Museum of Modern Art, 2008.

Kantor, Jordan. *Drawing from the Modern, 1975–2005.* New York: The Museum of Modern Art, 2005.

Lambrecht, Luc. "ForwArt." *Flash Art* 227 (November–December 2002): 41, 50.

Lange, Christy. "Arturo Herrera." *Frieze* 95 (November–December 2005): 142.

Lefkowitz, David. "Edgy: Painting at the Edge of the World at Walker Art Center." *New Art Examiner* 29, no. 1 (September–October 2001): 66–71, 103.

McCraken, David. "Blank Check." *Chicago Tribune,* March 4, 1994, 66.

McElheny, Josiah. "Arturo Herrera." *Bomb* 93 (Fall 2005): 68–75.

McFadden, Sarah. "ForwArt." *The Bulletin,* October 11, 2002.

McKenna, Max. "U.S. Artist Q&A, Arturo Herrera." *The Art Newspaper* (April 1998): 48.

MacKenzie, Duncan and Stephanie Smith. "Interview." *Proximity Magazine* (May–June, 2008): 24–27.

Mahler, Ute. "Das Atelier der Welt." *ART Das Kunstmagazin* (October 2006): 22–23.

Marcoci, Roxana. *Comic Abstraction: Image Breaking, Image Making.* New York: Museum of Modern Art, 2007.

Meschede, Friedrich. "Look: On the Collages of Arturo Herrera," in *Arturo Herrera: You Go First.* New York: D.A.P., 2005.

Meschede, Friedrich and Ingrid Schaffner in Maria do Céu Baptista, ed. *Arturo Herrera: 7 Abril–19 Xuño de 2005.* Santiago de Compostela: Centro Galego de Arte Contemporánea / Xunta de Galicia, 2005.

Molon, Dominic. "Arturo Herrera," in Thomas Bayrle, ed. *From Vitamin P: New Perspectives in Painting,* pp. 142–143. London: Phaidon, 2002.

Montreuil, Gregory. "Arturo Herrera / Brent Sikkema." *Flash Art* 118 (July–September 2002): 117–118.

Morgan, Jessica. "Arturo Herrera." *Grand Street* 66 (Fall 1998): 229.

Morgan, Nate. "'I do that.'" *Art:21 Blog,* January 28, 2009. http://blog.art21.org/2009/01/28/i-do-that/.

Müller, Hans-Joachim. *Frontside.* Basel: Friedrich Reinhardt, 2006.

Nakas, Kassandra, Ulrich Pfarr, and Andreas Schalhorn. *Funny Cuts: Cartoons and Comics in Contemporary Art.* New York: D.A.P., 2004.

The New Collage. New York: Pavel Zoubok Gallery, 2006.

Newhall, Edith. "On View: New York's New Art." *New York* Magazine, February 28, 2000, 76.

Olivares, Rosa. *100 artistas latinoamericanos = 100 Latin American Artists.* Barcelona: Exit, 2006.

Pace, Linda. *Dreaming Red: Creating ArtPace.* San Antonio, TX: ArtPace, 2003.

Patner, Andrew. "Arturo Herrera." *Chicago Sun Times,* January 29, 1998.

Pérez Oramas, Luis. *An Atlas of Drawings: Transforming Chronologies.* New York: Museum of Modern Art / D.A.P., 2006.

Phillips, Christopher. "Report from Istanbul: Band of Outsiders." *Art in America* (April 2000): 70–75.

"Play." Season 3. *Art:21 – Art in the Twenty-first Century.* DVD. Directed by Alexander Birchler and Teresa Hubbard. Alexandria, VA: Art 21, Inc. / PBS Home Video, 2005.

Prince, Nigel, ed. *Arturo Herrera.* Manchester: Cornerhouse, 2007.

Rangel, Gabriela. *Arturo Herrera*. Caracas: Sala Trasnocho Arte Contacto, 2009.

Rattemeyer, Christian. *The Judith Rothschild Foundation Contemporary Drawings Collection: Catalogue Raisonné*. New York: Museum of Modern Art, 2009.

"Rediscovering the Classics." *Art on Paper* 13, no. 4 (July–August 2008).

Rehberg, Vivian, ed. *Urgent Painting: 17 janvier–3 mars 2002*. Paris: Musée d'art moderne de la ville de Paris / Association Paris musées, 2002.

Schindler, Kelly. "Catherine Sullivan and Arturo Herrera In *Adaptation* in Chicago." *Art:21 Blog*, February 25, 2008. http://blog.art21.org/2008/02/25/catherine-sullivan-and-arturo-herrera-in-adaptation-in-chicago/

Schleifer, Kristen Brooke. "Trial by Fire." *New Art Examiner* 21, no. 9 (May 1994): 23–27.

Schuster, Robert. "Best in Show: Arturo Herrera's *Les Noces* at Americas Society." *The Village Voice*, February 24, 2011.

Sheets, Hilarie M. "The Big Draw." *ARTnews 106*, no. 1 (January 2006): 98–103.

Singer, Debra. *Arturo Herrera: Before We Leave: September 6–December 9, 2001*. New York: Whitney Museum of American Art, 2001.

Smith, Roberta. "Art in Review: Arturo Herrera." *New York Times*, May 17, 2002, p. E35.

________. "Visions That Flaunt Cartoon Pedigrees." *New York Times*, March 2, 2007.

Sogbe, Beatriz. "Arturo Herrera: Sala TAC." *Arte al día online*, April 11, 2010. http://www.artealdiaonline.com/International/Contenidos/Resenas/Arturo_Herrera.

Sollins, Marybeth and Susan. *Art 21: Art in the Twenty-First Century*. Vol. 3. New York: Harry N. Abrams, 2005.

Sudjic, Deyan. "Arturo Herrera." *Domus* 911 (Feb. 2008).

Tatar, Maria and Neville Wakefield. *Arturo Herrera*. Chicago: The Renaissance Society, 1998.

Taylor, Victor Zamudio. *Políticas de la diferencia. Arte iberoamericano fin de siglo*. Valencia: Generalitat Valenciana, 2001.

Trice, [illegible]. "Berliner Salon: Arturo Herrera at Galerie Max Hetzler." *Art:21 Blog*, April 4, 2008. http://blog.art21.org/2008/04/04/berliner-salon-arturo-herrera-at-galerie-max-hetzler/.

Vetrocq, Marcia E. "Arturo Herrera at Sikkema Jenkins." *Art in America* (April 2007).

Walker, Hamza. "Arturo Herrera : A Gentle Trauma." *The Renaissance Society Newsletter* (1998).

Wei, Lilly. "Twisting and Turning: Abstract Painting Now at Blue Star." *Voices of Art Magazine* 11, no. 2 (2003): 29–30.

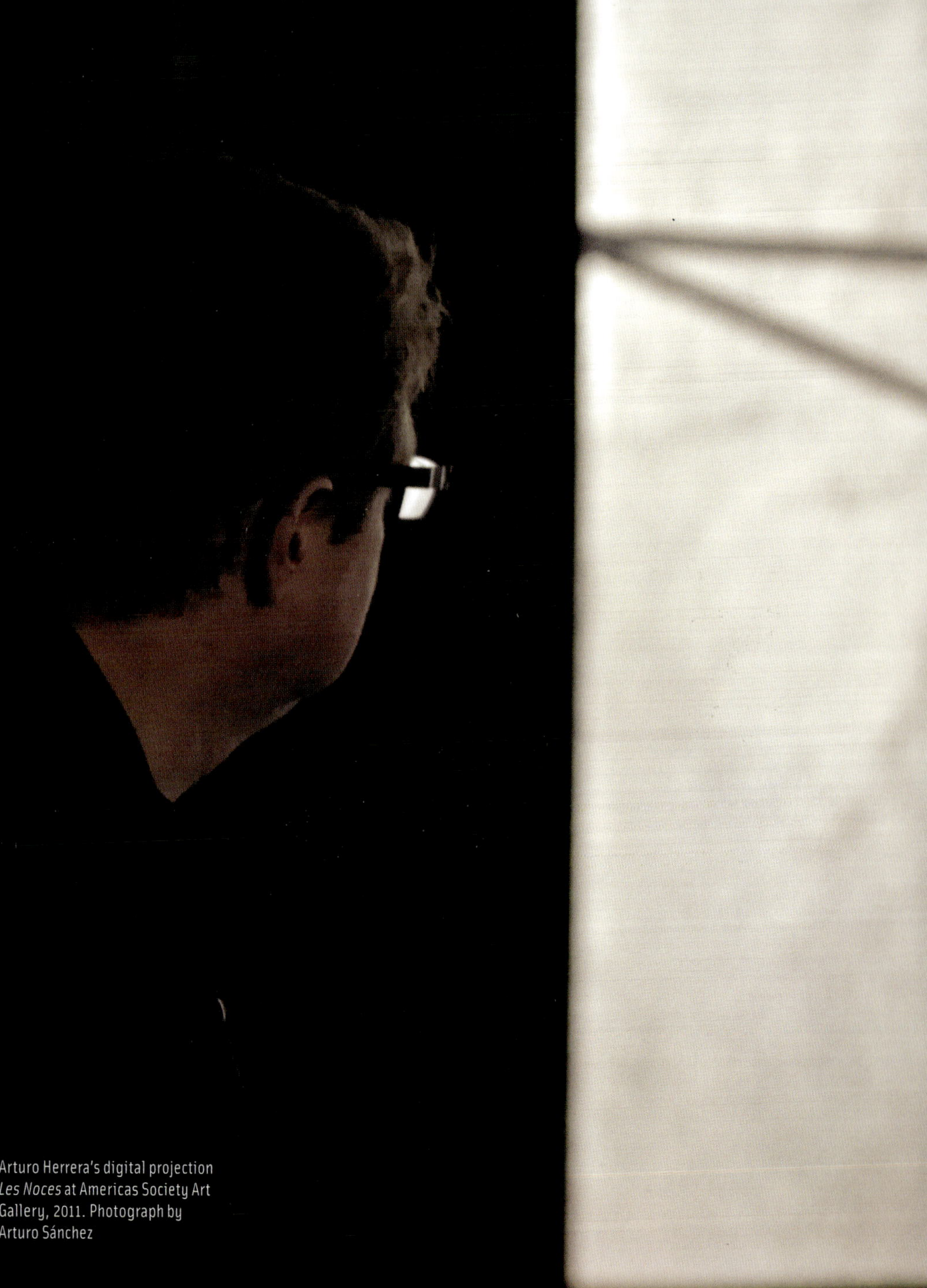

Arturo Herrera's digital projection *Les Noces* at Americas Society Art Gallery, 2011. Photograph by Arturo Sánchez

THE ARTIST AND EDITOR WISH TO THANK

Tiqui Atencio, Nuit Banai, Natalie Bunnell, British Broadcasting Corporation (BBC), Seth Decker, Estrellita and Daniel Brodsky, Bill Cooper, Christina De Leon, Sherry Dobbin, Lynn Garafola, Maria Cristina and Pablo Henning, Misi Breisacher Moshiri and Ali Moshiri, Michael Jenkins, Library of Congress, Dame Monica Mason, Gustavo Maturet, Ali Moshiri, Christopher Newton, Gabriela Rangel, Haleh Redjaian, Tahía Rivero, Lynne Rogers, Arturo Sánchez, Tarik Schirmer, Brent Sikkema, Victoria and Albert Museum, Isabela Villanueva, The Walt Disney Company, and Sebastian Zubieta

Americas Society is the premier organization dedicated to education, debate, and dialogue in the Americas. Its mission is to foster an understanding of the contemporary political, social, and economic issues confronting Latin America, the Caribbean, and Canada, and to increase public awareness and appreciation of the diverse cultural heritage of the Americas and the importance of the inter-American relationship.

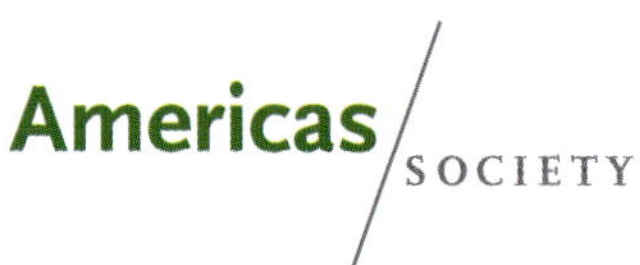

680 Park Avenue, New York, NY 10065
Phone: (212) 249-8950 Fax: (212) 249-5868
e-mail: artgallery@as-coa.org
Web site: www.as-coa.org/VisualArts

Cover: Arturo Herrera. Photographs from an untitled series, 2004. Gelatin silver prints, each 12 × 8 in. La Colección Jumex, Mexico City